Creativity, Mental Illness, and Crime

Second Edition

Russell Eisenman

Department of Psychology
University of Texas-Pan American
Edinburg, TX 78539-2999
E-mail: eisenman@utpa.edu

Kendall Hunt
publishing company

Cover image © Shutterstock, Inc.

Kendall Hunt
publishing company

www.kendallhunt.com
Send all inquiries to:
4050 Westmark Drive
Dubuque, IA 52004-1840

Copyright © 2007, 2011 by Russell Eisenman

ISBN 978-0-7575-9155-6

Printed in the United States of America
10 9 8 7 6 5 4 3 2

✖✖ Contents ✖✖

❈❈ Preface ❈❈

This book contains articles on important social issues. But, do not let the title throw you. This is not a book on whether or not creative people are mentally ill (although I discuss it some in chapter 12). Nor is it a book on whether or not creative people are often criminals. Rather, I deal with all the various topics in the title, plus additional chapters on such areas as drugs, schools, prisons, sex education, drug education, etc.

However, I do have a chapter on creativity in prisoners. It turns out that the romantic view of prisoners being creative people who end up in prison because society will not tolerate them is not supported. If there are creative criminals or prisoners they are probably in the minority, though some, no doubt, exist (for examples of creative prisoners see Eisenman, 2010).

Reference

Eisenman, R. (2010). Creativity and crime: How criminals use creativity to succeed. In D. H. Cropley, A. J. Cropley, J. C. Kaufman, & M. A. Runco (Eds.) *The dark side of creativity*. (pp. 204-217). New York: Cambridge University Press.

Creativity in Prisoners:
Conduct Disorders and Psychotics

XOX XOX XOX XOX XOX XOX XOX XOX XOX XOX XOX XOX XOX XOX

A neglected area of study is creativity in prisoners. One could make a case for prisoners being either high or low in creativity, and there would be treatment implications depending upon the conclusion. For example, Barron (1963) found that creative people often have anti-social tendencies, which is consistent with prisoners being creative, as they are very antisocial, for the most part. Creative people and prisoners are both unlikely to take authority at its word, but seek to challenge authority and look for their own solutions. Agnew (1989) has suggested that delinquency may develop as a creative enterprise for many adolescents. Of course, the antisocial nature of prisoners may be very different than the antisocial nature of, say, a creative artist. On the other hand, prisoners show uncreative tendencies in their rigidity and seeming inability to see alternatives to crime and aggression (Eisenman 1990b 1991). Many delinquents have overly aggressive ways of responding to a variety of situations (Dodge and Newman 1981; Guerra and Slaby 1990). Delinquents seem unable, much of the time, to see how they could achieve their end goals, other than by anti-social means (Platt and Spivack 1975).

The present study used two measures of creativity to assess creativity in conduct-disordered or psychotic prisoners in a facility for youthful offenders. The prisoners were mostly teenagers, with an age range of 14–24 years of age. The first method was preference for polygons varying in complexity-simplicity. Barron (1963) shows that creative people prefer complexity. The polygons used here were employed in much previous research, which showed their similarity to the Barron-Welsh Art Scale as a measure of creativity (Eisenman 1968a, 1968b, 1990a; Eisenman, Borod, and Grossman 1972;

Eisenman and Schussel 1970; Victor, Grossman, and Eisenman 1973). One advantage of using polygon preference as a creativity measure is that it is a nonverbal task and should be easy for subjects regardless of intelligence or educational level. This is especially important when working with prisoners, who tend to score very low on intellectual measures. For example, the prisoners in this study typically scored at about 85 on IQ tests and about six or seven grades below their proper level on achievement tests (e.g., prisoners who should be in the 12th grade typically scored at the 6th grade level in reading skills and the 5th grade level in mathematical skills).

The Thematic Apperception Test (TAT) (Morgan and Murray 1935) requires making up stories and thus calls upon verbal ability. However, in my work with the youthful offenders, I found that they tend to enjoy this test, perhaps because there are no right or wrong answers. A speech therapist at this prison said of the prisoners, "They like creative tasks, such as acting, painting, or story telling. They do not like typical school tasks." The TAT would seem to be consistent with the "creative" tasks she referred to and provided a second measure of creativity via ratings of stories, a method previously used (without the TAT) to assess creativity (Eisenman 1990a). There is some value in looking at creativity with more than one measure (Runco, in press-a, in press-b).

Method

Subjects

The participants were thirty prisoners diagnosed as conduct disorders and thirty prisoners diagnosed as having some kind of psychotic disorder. Fifteen of the conduct disorders were classified as solitary aggressive type, severe, while the other fifteen were classified as undifferentiated type, severe, indicating a mixture of clinical features including, possibly, conduct disorder within a group, such as gang activity. Sixteen of the psychotics were diagnosed with one of the schizophrenic disorders, while ten were considered psychotically depressed and four were diagnosed as manic-depressive. They were at a reception center where all youthful offenders in the state of California who live in the southern region are sent when they have been sentenced to imprisonment in the California Youth Authority. This is one of two facilities for processing new, male, youthful offenders in the state. The other is located in northern California. Also, as part of the reception center, but independent of it, there is an intensive treatment program where youthful offenders may stay for longer periods of time and receive psychotherapy. Fifteen of the subjects were obtained from the intensive treatment program while the other forty-five came from the reception center. The diagnoses were made after testing or assessment by Ph.D. clinical psychologists or by MSW social workers, all of whom had much experience working with this population. In ten instances where the original diagnosis was by an MSW social worker, the diagnosis was rechecked by a Ph.D. clinical psychologist, and there was complete agreement as to conduct disorder or psychotic, and 90% agreement as to specific subtypes, e.g., agreement that a prisoner was a manic-depressive psychotic.

Procedure

The prisoners were tested individually by an experimenter who was blind as to their diagnostic status. Half were administered the polygon preference test first, the other half the TAT first. Participants were told that they were taking tests that would provide information about their personality and that they would be given feedback. Both tests were administered in the same session, and prisoners were later given some feedback about their performance. Prisoners told stories to five TAT cards using standard TAT procedures (see below under Instruments) and chose their three most preferred polygons from a photograph of twelve polygons, which are described below.

Instruments

The polygons were twelve figures shown on a photograph, and varied from 4 to 24 points. Complexity is defined by the number of points or turns on the polygons. With these figures, points or turns will result in exactly the same score. Inward points are counted as well as the more obvious outward points. There were nine asymmetrical polygons with three each of 4, 12, and 24 points, and three symmetrical figures of 4, 8, and 10 points. However, a symmetrical polygon of 4 points is simpler than an asymmetrical polygon of 4 points, since one can predict half of it from viewing the other half, which is not the case with asymmetrical ones. The nine asymmetrical polygons were previously used by Vanderplas and Garvin (1959) and had originally been constructed by randomly connecting points on a 100 X 100 grid (Attneave and Arnoult 1957), i.e., there were 100 points on the grid and a random connecting of points was done to construct polygons. The symmetrical polygons were from Birkhoff (1933).

Prisoners chose their three most preferred shapes and it was decided, based of past research by the author, to have 40 points be the cut-off score for classification of "preference for complexity." That is, 40 or more points preference was taken as an indication of preference for complexity, while a complexity score of 39 or less (determined by adding up all the points on the three most preferred shapes) was deemed to indicate preference for simplicity. The rationale is that other procedures, such as a median split could result in some samples of participants being deemed to prefer complexity because they were in the upper 50% of their sample, when their actual scores were quite low, relative to what other people have chosen. So, an absolute standard was desired and 40 points was chosen as the cut-off because it seemed like a true preference for complexity. To obtain a score of 40, one would have to choose at least one of the highest complexity polygons, a 24-point figure. Then, if no other 24-point polygons were among the three most preferred, a participant would have to choose a middle-level complexity 12-point polygon, and could end up with a score of 40 by then choosing a 4-point figure. Thus, a cut-off score of 40 points assures that a complexity score will mean that the person viewing the 12 polygons used here chooses at least one of the highest level of complexity polygons and, if no other 24-point polygons are chosen, at least one mid-level complexity (12-point) polygon as well.

Five Thematic Apperception Test cards were used for the research: cards 1 (boy with violin), 4 (man pulling away from a woman), 8 BM (operation scene), 12 M (hypnosis scene), and 13 MF (man with woman; the woman is apparently nude and lying down). Prisoners were asked to tell stories indicating what was going on, what led up to it, and the outcome. To make clearer what was wanted the experimenter added that subjects should include the past, present, and future in their stories. Prisoners were also asked to tell the thoughts and feelings of everyone in the pictures. These are typical TAT instructions, often employed by clinical psychologists when giving the test. The results were scored by two independent scorers with previous experience in scoring stories for creativity research (Eisenman 1990a) and they had 92% agreement in scoring the presence or absence of creativity. Differences were resolved by discussion. The scorers did not know the diagnoses of the prisoners. The entire time to administer the two tests took less than an hour.

Results

For complexity-simplicity preferences in polygons, 12 of the 30 conduct disordered prisoners preferred complexity vs. only 2 of the 30 psychotics, as shown in Table 1.1 This yields a chi square of 7.24, df = 1, $p < .01$. Thus, while both groups of prisoners were more likely to prefer simplicity, and therefore choose like noncreative people, the psychotics were overwhelming in their preference for simplicity.

Table 1.1
Number of Conduct Disordered and Psychotic Prisoners Preferring Complex or Simple Polygons

| | Preference | |
	Complexity	Simplicity
Conduct Disorders	12	18
Psychotics	2	28

Note. $\chi^2(1) = 7.24$, $p < .01$

The choice of the prisoners was in a direction of simplicity much more than my previous research with high school or college students. Table 1.2 compares the prisoners with data obtained from students at a lower-class high school in California. The students from this high school had parents who were typically working class in occupations and who, mostly, had low incomes. These high school students were similar to the prisoners in social class, racial and ethnic makeup, and age. In both the prison and the high school, about 20% of the samples were white, 40% black, and 40% Hispanic. Also, most of the prisoners were of high school age, although a few were older. Almost all the prisoners were, like the high school students, from lower-class backgrounds, with perhaps four being upper-lower or lower-middle class, based on parents' occupation and income. Although only 30 of the seventy high school students preferred complexity, this finding is significant when compared with the overall prison sample's choice of fourteen preferring complexity and 46 preferring simplicity ($\chi^2(1) = 4.56, p < .05$ 1.

For ratings of the Thematic Apperception Test stories, 25 were rated creative and 19 of these were by conduct-disordered prisoners, whereas 6 were by psychotics. This yields a two-tailed binomial $p = .014$. Thus, conduct-disordered prisoners were significantly more likely to have their stories rated as creative than were the psychotic prisoners. Raters used criteria of originality and usefulness in the sense of not rating a story as creative if it were simply bizarre or incoherent. An interesting qualitative finding is that the stories rated as creative tended to be about crime.

Table 1.2
Number of High School Students and Prisoners Preferring Complexity or Simplicity

| | Preference | |
	Complexity	Simplicity
High School Students	30	40
Prisoners	14	46

Note. $\chi^2(1) = 4.56, p < .05$.

Discussion

The findings suggest that prisoners are low in creativity. This is true whether we look at complexity-simplicity preferences in polygons or whether we look at rated creativity on the Thematic Apperception Test. Also, psychotics were lower in creativity than the conduct-disordered prisoners. Recently, research has suggested that under some circumstances there may be a positive link between creativity and mental illness (Andreasen 1987; Flach 1990). The findings of the present study are in the opposite direction: psychotic prisoners were lower in creativity than conduct-disordered prisoners and were also lower in creativity than the lower class high school students. Psychosis, thus, does not necessarily correlate positively with creativity. Perhaps there is a link between creativity and psychosis in people with highly creative skills, but for the average person (Eisenman 1990a) or for prisoners the link may be in the opposite direction. Also, the link may perhaps be strongest when the psychosis is manic depression (Andreasen 1987), while in the present study the greatest number of psychotic prisoners were schizophrenic. I would doubt, however, that a sample of manic depressive prisoners would be high in creativity. I suspect that it is already creative people with hypomania who manifest the link between mental illness and creativity. This is, of course, an empirical question, to be answered by data collection.

The results have treatment implications for prisoners. It is difficult to treat prisoners and one reason may be that they have severe limitations in grasping concepts. This limitation, which I experienced in doing psychotherapy with prisoners, may be, in part, due to low creativity as well as other more obvious reasons, such as low intelligence. Golann (1962) noted that while creative people like independence, low creative people prefer assigned, familiar tasks. This may explain something which I observed during my twenty-one months of prison work, and which was quite amazing: prison does not seem so unpleasant to criminals. It is not just institutionalization, but the fact that the prison provides a structure appealing to low creative people. The authoritarian structure of the prison is reassuring to the low creative prisoner, in contrast to the ambiguity of life in free society. Thus, prisons may not deter crime because imprisonment is not deemed that negative by criminals.

The prisoners seemed to be most creative when telling stories about crime on the Thematic Apperception Test, and least creative when telling stories that were not antisocial. They seem to utilize what creativity they do have for criminal purposes. Often, in conducting therapy with them, I was impressed with the clever ideas prisoners came up with to commit crimes or to keep from getting caught. However, this same cleverness, or creativity, was not applied in learning how to function non-criminally in society. It would be interesting to know if non-apprehended criminals show the same low creativity as the prisoners in the present sample. One could argue that criminals who get caught are low in creativity but perhaps the successful ones are high in creativity. However, many of the prisoners were successful criminals for quite some time, but eventually got caught as they kept committing crimes. So there may not be the great difference between currently non-imprisoned criminals and currently imprisoned ones that one is, at first blush, tempted to suspect.

Based on the present findings, treatment for prisoners might focus on highly structured, directive therapy sessions in which the therapist makes clear what is "the right way." Instead of being non-directive or leaving choices up to the prisoner, it might be wise, given their low creativity, to make clear what skills and choices are desirable and then help them learn to achieve these things.

Some limitations of the study need to be considered. First, the scoring system for rating the Thematic Apperception Test stories emphasized usefulness as well as originality. This may have worked against the psychotic prisoners, who sometimes told stories that seemed pointless or incoherent. A more liberal scoring system, which gave credit for such stories, could call some of them creative. While this was considered undesirable, one could argue that bizarreness and incoherence may be associated with creativity and should thus be accepted. The present scoring procedure tended not to count stories lacking coherence or sense as being creative. Second, the findings are based on samples at one prison. Other prisons may have different kinds of inmates and this could possibly lead to different conclusions. For example, to be incarcerated in the California Youth Authority, one has to have a long record of arrests or to have committed an extremely serious crime such as rape, attempted murder, etc. Most of the prisoners fell into the first category, having long criminal careers, even though most were in their teens. Third, it seems likely that the great thought disorganization of the psychotic prisoners inhibited their creativity. Perhaps this would have been less so if there had been more manic-depressives in the psychotic group, and fewer schizophrenics and psychotic depressives. Both schizophrenia and psychotic depression might cause greater incapacitation of thought than manic-depression, especially for manic-depressives who are not currently experiencing a full-blown manic or depressive state.

References

Andreasen, N. C. 1987. Creativity and mental illness: Prevalence rates in writers and their first-degree relatives. *American Journal of Psychiatry, 144*, 1288–1292.

Attneave, F., and M. D. Arnoult. 1956. Methodological considerations in the quantitative study of shape and pattern in perception. *Psychological Bulletin, 53*, 452–471.

Barron, F. 1963. *Creativity and psychological health.* Princeton, NJ: Van Nostrand.

Birkhoff, G. D. 1933. *Aesthetic measure.* Cambridge, MA: Harvard University Press.

Dodge, K. A., and P. J. Newman. 1981. Biased decision-making processes in aggressive boys. *Journal of Abnormal Psychology, 90*, 375–379.

Flach, F. 1990. Disorders of the pathways involved in the creative process. *Creativity Research Journal, 3*, 158–165.

Golann, S. L. 1962. The creativity motive. *Journal of Personality, 30*, 588–600.

Guerra, N. G., and R. G. Slaby. 1990. Cognitive mediators of aggression in adolescent offenders: 2. Intervention. *Developmental Psychology, 26*, 269–277.

Eisenman, R. 1968a. Complexity-simplicity and reaction to threatening information. *Journal of Consulting and Clinical Psychology, 32*, 638–641.

———. 1968b. Personality and demography in complexity-simplicity. *Journal of Consulting and Clinical Psychology, 32*, 140–143.

———. 1990a. Creativity, preference for complexity, and physical and mental illness. *Creativity Research Journal, 3*, 233–238.

———. 1990b. Six problems of a prison psychologist: A personal account. *Psychological Reports, 67*, 755–761.

———. 1991. I worked in a prison: An insider's story. *Psychology: A Journal of Human Behavior, 28*, (3 and 4), 22–26.

———., J. Borod, and J. C. Grossman. 1972. Sex differences in the interrelationships of authoritarianism, anxiety, creative attitudes, preference for complex polygons, and the Barron-Welsh Art Scale. *Journal of Clinical Psychology, 28*, 549–550.

———. and N. R. Schussel. 1970. Creativity, birth order and preference for symmetry. *Journal of Consulting and Clinical Psychology, 34*, 275–280.

Morgan, C. D., and H. A. Murray. 1935. A method for investigating fantasies: The Thematic Apperception Test. *Archives of Neurology and Psychiatry, 34*, 289–306.

Platt, J. J., and G. Spivak. 1975. *Manual for the means-ends problem-solving procedure (MEPS): A measure of interpersonal cognitive problem-solving skill.* Philadelphia: Hahnemann Medical College and Hospital.

Runco, M. A. In press-a, ed. *Divergent thinking.* Norwood, NJ: Ablex.

———. In press-b, ed. *Problem finding, problem solving, and creativity.* Norwood, NJ: Ablex.

Vanderplas, J. M., and E. A. Garvin. 1959. The association value of random shapes. *Journal of Experimental Psychology, 57*, 147–154.

Victor, H. R., R. Eisenman, and J. C. Grossman. 1973. Openness to experience and marijuana use in high school students. *Journal of Consulting and Clinical Psychology, 41*, 78–85.

Why We Need the Death Penalty

XOX XOX XOX XOX XOX XOX XOX XOX XOX XOX XOX XOX XOX XOX

Before I began working with youthful offenders in a state prison treatment program, I was in favor of the death penalty. After such work, I am even more in favor of the death penalty. Most hard-core criminals cannot be rehabilitated, at least not with the skills we now possess. For the protection of society, we need long sentences for the truly dangerous ones, and the death penalty for many murderers. At least 9% of murderers on death row have killed previously (i.e., have a conviction for a homicide preceding the one for which they were sentenced to death), and about 7% of murderers released from prison are known to kill again. Also, people convicted of homicide (murder or non-negligent manslaughter) typically serve less than seven years in prison, even if sentenced to life imprisonment.[1] Had these killers been executed for their first murder, hundreds of lives would have been saved. As time goes on, the number of people murdered by second-time murderers will go into the thousands.

It is important that the death penalty not be dragged out for many years, or this reduces any deterrent effect, except on those executed. However, do not forget that the above cited information means that the deterrent effect on those executed is most important—many lives will be saved by preventing that person from committing future murders. Also, beyond the issue of murder, my experience is that the hard-core offenders I worked with typically bring much misery into the lives of others via their many crimes. So even if a murderer is released from prison and never commits another murder, he may commit burglaries, assaults, rapes, etc. The person who is law abiding and kills, say, a loved one in a moment of passion may be unlikely to reoffend (and perhaps should not be executed) although even here caution is needed. Often, the killer of the loved one is a violent person who would likely do the same thing again, or is a criminally oriented person whom the authorities have not captured, but who has committed swindles, embezzlements, assaults, etc. As pointed out by Bidinotto, swifter and more effective punishment for crimes would be more likely to have a deterrent effect than the system we typically have now.[2]

Illogical Arguments Against Capital Punishment

The arguments against the death penalty are often emotional and illogical. For example, it is often said that the United States has one of the highest rates of executions and imprisonment of any civilized nation. Often South Africa and the Soviet Union are cited as being our bedfellows in the high rate of executions or imprisonment. The illogical arguments here are the attempts to make it seem that since most civilized societies do not do something it must be wrong, and since South Africa and the Soviet Union are often thought of in negative terms, to be like them in any way must be wrong. A similar emotional, illogical argument is to point out that the death penalty in the United States is highest in the South. Here, the argument is that we should think of the South in negative terms and thus the death penalty should be thought of negatively. This makes no sense, other than in terms of using the South as a scapegoat for our nation's ills[3] and assuming that anything southern is bad. In my experience, people in the South are friendlier than people in many other sections of our nation. Does that mean that friendliness is bad because it occurs disproportionately in the South? Or, warm weather? Of course not.

Another dubious argument against capital punishment is what I call the "exceptions" argument, which says all kinds of exceptions should be made: i.e., the youth of the offender, brain damage, drug addiction, or past sexual abuse to the offender. In all these cases, we should have some sympathy for the offender based on their horrible circumstances, but it does not make them less likely to kill again. In fact, any or all of the above may make them more likely to kill again or commit more crimes. Sympathy should not be equated with excusing the behavior.

Humanitarian Concerns

People who favor capital punishment sometimes come across as low in humanitarian concerns. We should not allow the need for capital punishment to make us disregard fundamental, humanitarian concepts. Many of these fundamental concepts are embedded in the American values and legal system, such as treating others fairly, the right to a fair trial, the right of appeal, etc. If the death penalty is being applied *unfairly* against a racial or ethnic group, then that is wrong. Just having a disproportionate amount of death penalties inflicted on a group is not, per se, evidence of unfair treatment, since that group may be committing a disproportionate amount of murders. But, if real bias can be shown, then corrective action is needed.

Regarding youth, we have a tradition in America of excusing youthful behavior, but we need to be less excusing. I worked with youthful offenders, and many of them were vicious and lacked remorse. They were very dangerous. Some of them could be reformed, but many of them could not. A juvenile committing murder should not necessarily escape the death penalty due to his or her age. The same thing applies to imprisonment: it is a mistake to let highly criminal youth off the hook with just a slap on the wrist, since some of them are the very people who commit an incredibly disproportionate amount of crime.[4]

Conclusion

We need the death penalty. Whether or not it has a deterrent effect on the general population is in dispute, but it certainly deters the criminals executed, which will save hundreds or thousands of innocent lives. Life imprisonment without parole would be a possible effective alternative to the death penalty; but the trouble is that we typically do not impose it; and even if it were imposed, prisoners could escape or might have their sentences commuted. Also, while in prison they can attack staff and other prisoners, making life miserable for many. As Bidinotto noted, punishment must be swifter then it typically is, if it is to be effective. This applies both to the speed of imprisonment for crimes and the need for swifter executions of convicted murderers.

Notes

1. Data from Bureau of Justice Statistics, United States Department of Justice. See, especially, the following reports: *Sourcebook of Criminal Justice Statistics—1991*, NCJ–137639, 1992; "Prison admissions and releases, 1983," NCJ–00582, March 1966; "Sentencing outcomes in 28 felony courts, 1986," NCJ–05743, August 1987; *1990 directory of automated criminal justice information systems, Vol. 4, Probation and parole; and Report to the nation on crime and justice. (Second edition)*, NCJ–105506, June 1988.
2. Robert James Bidinotto, "Swifter Punishment Would Reduce Violence," in Janelle Rohr editor, *Violence in America*, (San Diego, CA: Greenhaven Press, 1990), pp. 266–273. Originally published in *The Freeman*, July 1989 and Sept. 1989.
3. Russell Eisenman, *From Crime to Creativity: Psychological and Social Factors in Deviance*. (Dubuque, IA: Kendall-Hunt, 1991). See also the chapter on crime for an overview of why people become criminals and what their attitudes are.
4. Donald Hanks, *Selective Incapacitation: Preventive Detention of the Violent Offender*. (New York: Vantage Press, 1991).

Student Attitudes toward David Duke before and after Seeing the Film, "Who Is David Duke?"

※◎※ ※◎※ ※◎※ ※◎※ ※◎※ ※◎※ ※◎※ ※◎※ ※◎※ ※◎※ ※◎※ ※◎※ ※◎※ ※◎※

David Duke is one of the most interesting politicians of recent times. A former head of the Ku Klux Klan and a former Nazi sympathizer, he has denied his racist past, and says he has changed. He is a member of the Louisiana House of Representatives and ran a strong race for the United States Senate, in which he gained about 45% of the total vote and more than 50% of the white vote in Louisiana (Eisenman 1992). A study of why people like him may throw light on the psychology of prejudice or on how attitudes are formed. Duke's denial of his past is a clever position, as it allows people to say they are for him without having to admit to holding racist attitudes. It makes sense for a person with some stigma in their past to deny that they currently have the stigma (Eisenman 1991; Goffman 1963; Jones, Farina, Hastorf, Markus, Miller, and Scott 1984). Yet, Duke's constant attack on blacks, using code terms such as "welfare cheats" allows one to hold to an implicit racist view without overt acknowledgement. Today, it is usually not acceptable to be overtly racist in the United States, although indirect expression is often prevalent.

Although Duke claims he is not a racist or a Nazi and no longer sympathizes with such people, the Public Broadcasting System film *Who is David Duke?* shown on the program *Frontline*, provides a different picture. In this film, people say that when they talk with Duke in private, a totally different view of him emerges, in contrast with his public stance of not being a prejudiced person. In private, people say, he condemns blacks and Jews, says the Holocaust never happened, and advised a Nazi to be less obvious in what he is saying. This advice to the Nazi would seem to indicate that Duke may be following the same path: he has exchanged his Ku Klux Klan robes and overt hatred for a business suit and a disguised racism. Would students who see this film change in their views of Duke? A previous study indicated that just over 50% of students in a Louisiana university liked Duke (Eisenman 1992). If similar findings are obtained before viewing the film, perhaps the content of the film will cause a change in their view of Duke. On the other hand, much of his appeal seems to be more emotional than ideological, with whites seeing him as something of a savior for them, especially in a state suffering economic poverty due to the decline of the previously prosperous oil industry. If an emotional appeal is the basis of his popularity, then perhaps the film would have little or no effect.

Method

Subjects

The participants were ninety-four students at a state university in Louisiana. These students were in a large Introduction to Psychology class, from the same university as were students in the previous study (Eisenman 1992), who were also in an Introduction to Psychology class.

Method

Students indicated like or dislike of David Duke on a sheet of paper, answering "Yes" or "No" to the question, "Is he a racist?" both before and after seeing the Public Broadcasting System film *Who is David Duke?*, which was originally shown on the program *Frontline*. Since the film is one hour long and the class meets for fifty minutes, the film was shown over two consecutive class periods, which allowed time for both the showing of the film and the answering of the two questions. The students also were asked to indicate their gender: male or female, and their race: black, white, or Oriental. There were thirty-nine white females in the class, thirty-eight white males, eleven black females, three black males, one Oriental male, one white who failed to list gender, and one student who listed neither gender nor race.

Results

All statistical results reported are two-tailed binomial tests. The major finding was that students tended not to change their views after watching the film. Those who liked Duke beforehand liked him afterwards, and vice versa. Specifically, only 23% of women and 8% of men showed any negative change toward Duke after watching the film, with negative change being defined as indicating either dislike after having first indicated "like" or "yes he is a racist" after previously indicating "no he is not a racist." Only nine of thirty-nine white females showed any change of this nature and only three of thirty-eight white males. Thus, the attitudes tended to remain the same ($p < .01$). All black students and the one Oriental male indicated dislike of Duke and answered yes to the racist question both before and after the film ($p < .01$). Specifically, five women changed from like to dislike after the film and five changed from no on racism to yes on racism after seeing the film. For men, one changed to dislike after the film and two changed to yes on racism. Surprisingly, a few students changed in the direction of being more positive to Duke after seeing the film. One white student who did not list gender changed from disliking Duke and seeing him as a racist to liking Duke and seeing him as not being racist. One white female changed from dislike of Duke before the film to like afterwards, and one white male who listed himself as undecided on both the like-dislike and racist-no racist questions changed to "like" and "not a racist" after viewing the film.

Seeing Duke as racist did not necessarily mean that students disliked him. Eight of thirty-nine white females and eight of thirty-eight white males said, before seeing the film, that they liked Duke and considered him racist. Before seeing the film, seven of the thirty-nine white females who liked Duke said he is not racist. For the male students, fifteen of the thirty-eight white men indicated that they liked Duke and considered him not racist.

Discussion

The results show that even though the film *Who is David Duke?* seemed to expose Duke as anti-black, anti-Semitic, and pro-Nazi, students who had favorable attitudes toward him before the film maintained their views after seeing the film. At least some of these students are likely overt racists themselves, as indicated by those who say they like Duke even though they see him as a racist. Others may be covert racist, and find Duke's statements to their liking. Of course, before a film or any persuasive message can have an effect it must be perceived. It is possible that these young students did not understand the film, did not pay attention, or otherwise missed the message. Others may have been so racist or so pro-Duke that they got the message but rejected it. In a discussion after the research, some students said that they were not racist and that they liked what Duke said about some things even though he may be racist and they may not like all that he says or stands for. This position is either (a) a rationalization or (b) consistent with the view that these students are basically non-ideological, and find Duke to their liking because of his charismatic appeal. Duke is young (aided in his appearance by plastic surgery) and comes across as not your typical politician. People seem to have a negative view of government (Katz, Gutek, Kahn, and Barton, 1975; Sirgo and Eisenman 1990), so someone who runs for political office as an outsider (not the typical politician) may have much appeal. This may explain, at least in part, the appeal of Texas billionaire H. Ross Perot in his 1992 bid for the presidency of the United States. Some people seem to like a non-typical politician even though they know little of what he stands for.

Duke's appeal would seem to reflect a new kind of prejudice, different from the overt prejudice and racism of the authoritarian personality (Adorno, Frenkel-Brunswik, Levinson, and Sanford 1950) but having much in common with it. Duke and his followers can deny being overtly prejudiced but still maintain views critical of marginalized groups in the United States: blacks, the poor, people on welfare, and criminals. Duke's campaign statements have attacked all these groups, and such attacks may serve a scapegoat function for people who feel threatened by bad economic times in the state, and their perception that blacks get special breaks from the government, such as affirmative action hiring (*Lake Charles American Press* 1991). Also, anti-black attitudes may often coincide with support for conservative candidates (Eisenman and Sirgo 1992).

The support for Duke found in the present sample was just over 50% for the white students, which is consistent with (a) a previous study at the same university, which also used Introduction to Psychology students (Eisenman 1992), and (b) his actual white vote in the 1990 United States Senate race, which he lost getting about 45% of the total vote in Louisiana but getting about 55% of the white vote (Freemantle 1990). Thus, these students may accurately reflect how people in Louisiana feel toward Duke.

References

Adorno, T. W., E. Frenkel-Brunswik, D. J. Levinson, and R. N. Sanford. 1950. *The authoritarian personality*. New York: Harper and Row.

Eisenman, R. 1992. Creativity, social and political attitudes, and liking or disliking David Duke. *Bulletin of the Psychonomic Society*, 30, 19–22.

————., and H. B. Sirgo. 1992, March. *Racial attitudes and voting behavior in the 1988 national elections.* Paper presented at the annual meeting of the Southwestern Social Science Association, Austin, TX.

Freemantle, T. 1990, October 8. Strong finish indicates Duke is future force. *Houston Chronicle*, pp. 1A, 6A.

Goffman, E. 1963. *Stigma*. Englewood Cliffs, NJ: Prentice-Hall.

Jones, E. E., A. Farina, A. H. Hastorf, H. Markus, D. T. Miller, and R. A. Scott. 1984. Social stigma: *The psychology of marked relationships*. New York: W. H. Freeman.

Katz, D., E. Barton, B. A. Gutkek, and R. L. Kahn. 1975. *Bureaucratic encounters: A pilot study of evaluation of government service*. Ann Arbor, MI: Institute for Social Research.

Lake Charles American Press, "Many turning to Duke out of frustration, pollster says," March 27, 1991, p. 10.

Sirgo, H. B., and R. Eisenman. 1990. Perceptions of governmental fairness by liberals and conservatives. *Psychological Reports*, 67, 1331–1334.

Academic Performance in Reading a Text as Related to Course Grades: Student Performance When Studying Is Impossible

XOX XOX XOX XOX XOX XOX XOX XOX XOX XOX XOX XOX XOX XOX

Building on the research of Kulhavy, Yekovich, and Dyer (1976, 1979) about feedback and learning, Stock, Winston, Behrens, and Harper-Marinick (1989) developed a cognitive discrepancy model to explain certain aspects of student performance. Looking at text study time, the authors believe that a continuous feedback loop occurs to reduce the discrepancy between what the student expects to perform and what feedback shows to be the actual performance. Study time would increase when students perform below their expectation.

There is, however, another explanation for student performance, which has nothing to do with study time or cognitions about discrepancy. This other explanation is that some students are high in ability and others are low. This ability could be general intelligence, reasoning skills, reading ability, certain kinds of intelligence—or whatever (Howard Gardner quoted in Goleman, Kaufman and Ray 1992). The prediction from this view would be that the high ability students achieve well academically and the low ability students do not. To test this assumption and to distinguish it from the Stock et al. (1989) model, it would be necessary to have a situation in which academic performance is assessed but studying is impossible. This was done in the present study, with the results of text reading compared to grades at the end of the semester.

The co-authors are Cam L. Melville and Connie F. St. Andrie from McNeese State University, Lake Charles, Louisiana.

Method

Subjects

The subjects were sixty-eight undergraduate students enrolled in an Introduction to Psychology class at a state university. The university has open admissions, which means that a wide range of ability is present in the lower division courses, such as Introduction to Psychology, which has mostly freshman and sophomore students.

Procedure

The instructor informed the students that they could get points on their final grade by participating in the study. The students were told that everyone who participated would get one point added to their final grade. For example, if their final grade was 79 and they participated in the study, their final grade would be 80. However, they were told that additional, unspecified amounts of points would be added to the final grade depending on how well they performed on the test to be given by the experimenters. The better the performance, the more points would be added. This information should have provided the students with motivation to take the task seriously and try to do well.

The task involved reading material passed out by the experimenters, which consisted of five different sections of five and one-half pages from the chapter on social psychology in the students' textbook, which was Gerow (1989). The five different sections were cohesive in and of themselves, but were not in the order in which Gerow had written them. Also, different orders were given to different students, so cheating would be minimized or impossible. The entire reading time was twenty-five minutes, as there was five minutes allowed per section, which were passed out one section at a time. The social psychology chapter had not been covered in the class, so it was material the student had not previously read. There were thirty multiple choice questions, six per section, used by the experimenters, taken from the instructor's test manual, which accompanies Gerow (1989). The students were allowed as much time as they needed to answer the thirty questions (within the limits of the class period, which met for fifty minutes) and most finished in fifteen to twenty minutes.

The final grades for the course were based on the traditional 10-point spread, with A being 90–100%, B = 80–89%, C = 70–79%, D = 60–69%, and F being less than 60%. There were also six students in the sample who later withdrew from the course and thus obtained a W for withdrawal.

Results

All the statistical probabilities reported are two-tailed binomial tests obtained from the table in Siegel (1956) but doubled, since he reports one-tailed probabilities. We looked at students scoring 70% and above on the 30-item text reading test versus students who scored below 70%. As expected, the students whose final course grades were A did very well on the 30-item test. All six A students scored above 70% versus none who scored below 70% correct ($p = .032$). Five of the A students scored in the 70–79% range, while one scored in the 80s. Also as expected, the F students did extremely poorly. All seven of them scored below 60% on the 30-item test ($p = .016$). Scores below 70% also predominated for the students whose final grades were D, W, or B. For D students, all 15 scored below 70% on the text test ($p = .002$), for students who later withdrew five of six scored below 70% ($p = .032$), and for the B students thirteen of seventeen scored below 70% ($p = .05$). The only grade group which did not reach the .05 level was the C students, where ten scored below 70% and seven scored above ($p = .630$).

Discussion

The results are consistent with expectation, with the possible exception of the B students who performed poorly on the text reading test. Otherwise A students performed well, and students who made D, F, or W (withdrew from the course) performed poorly. The findings are consistent with the view that we do not always need to say that studying, feedback, expectations, discrepancy, etc. are necessary to explain academic achievement. In this investigation, students could not study for the test, but the results were consistent with their final grade, suggesting that some overall ability factor(s) controlled performance in the text reading test. The results do not disprove Stock et al. (1989), but suggest that there are different paths to the same endpoint, in this case academic performance. Their cognitive model no doubt explains student performance in some cases, while the ability explanation advanced here also explains student achievement. Thus, the two explanations can be seen as complementary. At times, people use feedback and decide to increase their studying (or work output) to achieve the level of performance they have come to expect. But at other times their ability allows them to achieve, independent of study, increased output, expectation, or similar concepts.

The fact that the B students performed not like the A students but more like the D, F, or W students is a little puzzling, since we tend to think of B as a good grade—not as good as A but in roughly the same domain. However, it may be that the course was graded in a relatively easy fashion, so that getting a B was not all that difficult. Or it may be that the kind of ability needed to do well on the reading text test has to be very high, so that even students who could attain a B do not possess that ability. Only the A students do.

The fact that the study was done at an open admissions university may be important. Someone who repeats the study at a more selective school may not get the same results, since Detterman (1986; Detterman and Daniel 1989) has shown that it is important to have subjects with a wide range of cognitive or intellectual functioning. Many variables can affect academic performance (Eisenman 1992; in press), and using a wide range of subject ability is more likely to show the true effects than using a sample restricted in range of cognitive or intellectual ability. This is a measurement truism, but may be especially true for the kind of ability assessed here.

References

Detterman, D. K. 1986, November. *Basic cognitive processes predict IQ.* Paper presented at the Psychonomic Society, New Orleans, LA.

————., and M. H. Daniel. 1989. Correlations of mental tests with each other and with cognitive variables are highest for low IQ groups. *Intelligence, 13*, 349–359.

Eisenman, R. 1992. *Academic achievement in high school of blacks and whites: A retrospective study of freshmen college students who would not have been admitted without open admissions*. Unpublished manuscript, McNeese State University.

————. In press. Creativity and impulsivity: The deviance perspective. In W. McCown, M.B. Shure, and J. Johnson, eds. *The impulsive client: Theory, research, and treatment*. Washington, DC: American Psychological Association.

Gerow. J. R. 1989. *Psychology: An introduction* (2nd edit). Glenview: Scott Foresman.

Goleman, D., P. Kaufman, and M. Ray. 1992. *The creative spirit*. New York: Dutton.

Kulhavy, R. W., J. W. Dyer, and F. R. Yekovich. 1976. Feedback and response confidence. *Journal of Educational Psychology, 68*, 522–528.

————. 1979. Feedback and content review in programmed instruction. *Contemporary Educational Psychology, 4*, 91–98.

Siegel, S. 1956. *Nonparametric statistics for the behavioral sciences*. New York: McGraw-Hill.

Stock, W. A., I. T. Behrens, M. Harper-Marinick, and K. S. Winston. 1989. The effects of performance expectation and question difficulty on text study time, response certitude, and correct responding. *Bulletin of the Psychonomic Society, 27*, 567–569.

Availability of Drugs in Our Schools as Related to Student Characteristics

Information from The National Crime Victimization Survey

XOX XOX XOX XOX XOX XOX XOX XOX XOX XOX XOX XOX XOX XOX

What are the characteristics of students who find drugs available in the primary and secondary schools? This is an important question and, fortunately, there is information available, although most people do not know of it nor realize that the data is accessible. The United States Department of Justice, through its Bureau of Justice Statistics, provides information on a variety of justice-related issues. One such effort is the National Crime Victimization Survey, which deals with a variety of issues (Bureau of Justice Statistics 1990a, 1990b, 1991a, 1991b, 1991c). The data reported in this article is also available in computerized form, along with additional data, from the National Archive of Criminal Justice Data, University of Michigan, and the Director of the Bureau of Justice Statistics, Steven D. Dillingham, has encouraged scholars to explore the data further. The present article is based on a Bureau of Justice Statistics (1991c) report involving a nation-wide survey of 47,000 households conducted in 1990 in which various questions about victimization were asked. The results are surprising as to what kinds of students are most exposed to drugs in the schools. In this study, students were not asked about alcohol. There was an impressive 98% response rate. Students are reporting their perceptions of drug availability, not their personal use of drugs.

The co-author is William Kritsonis from McNeese State University.

It is generally assumed that the kinds of youth most exposed to drugs are inner-city, minority youth who come from backgrounds of extreme poverty (*Hip-Hop Generation* 1992; MEE Productions, 1992). When I worked in a prison (Eisenman 1991a) this was exactly the typical prisoner, and most had been involved in drug usage—some quite heavily. So the data from the national survey reported here have some surprising conclusions.

Results

Table 5.1 shows student characteristics and availability of drugs in the schools, as reported by respondents in the nation-wide survey. The amazing finding is that it is not black or Hispanic youth who find drugs most available in the schools, nor is it poor youth. It is wealthy, white, non-Hispanics who reported the greatest availability of drugs in their schools. Also, it is not the inner-city schools (referred to as central city in the table) where drugs are reported to be most available, nor is it even the suburban schools. Rather, drug availability in the schools is reported most available in the non-metropolitan area schools. These schools are not located within the U. S. Census Bureau classification of a Metropolitan Statistical Area, which is a county or group of counties containing at least one city or combined cities of 50,000 or more inhabitants. Thus, non-metropolitan schools would include the rural and small town schools, isolated from any big city.

All of the above findings are contrary to most expectations. Other findings are more in accord with expectations: drugs are most available in the schools to males and to older students. While we must exercise caution whenever dealing with self report, the findings may have some validity, as illustrated in the following vignette.

Table 5.1
Availability of drugs by selected student characteristics

Student characteristic	Total	Available	Not available	Not known if available
Sex				
Male	100%	69%	12%	19%
Female	100	66	11	22
Race				
White	100%	69%	11%	20%
Black	100	67	11	22
Other	100	58	18	16
Hispanic origin				
Hispanic	100%	64%	12%	24%
Non-Hispanic	100	68	11	20
Not ascertained	100	52	31	16
Age				
12	100%	53%	24%	23%
13	100	60	19	21
14	100	64	13	24
15	100	70	7	23
16	100	76	6	18
17	100	77	6	17
18	100	78	6	16
19	100	78	5	17
Family income				
Less than $15,000	100%	67%	13%	20%
$15,000–$29,999	100	68	11	21
$30,000–$49,999	100	68	11	21
$50,000 or more	100	70	11	18
Not ascertained	100	66	13	21
Location of residence				
Central city	100%	66%	13%	21%
Suburbs	100	67	11	22
Non-metro area	100	71	11	18

The columns are headed "Percent of students reporting drugs".

Note: Detail may not total 100% because of rounding. Cases in which the respondent did not know the types of drugs were excluded. "Available" includes students who said drugs were easy or hard to get at school; "not available" includes those saying drugs were impossible to get at school.

A Case History

While the above findings seem amazing, they are consistent with an experience one of us had working with a single-parent, white woman whose daughter went to an upper-class high school in a small city. The mother was divorced and from a lower-middle-class background, and was so happy to get her daughter into the "good" school. It had many wealthy students, mostly white in contrast to the other schools in town, which were racially mixed or almost all black. We were not sure if the mother somehow lived in the school district for the "good" school or if she pulled some strings to get her daughter in. The daughter, Debbie, was a 16-year old who was now to be exposed to good teachers, smart students, and a school with all the modern technology, in contrast to the other, poorer high schools in the city.

What happened was that Debbie started losing weight rapidly, and went from 115 pounds to 90 pounds in the course of a few months. While an eating disorder may have been present, the cause that we know of was drug usage. It seems that many students in this "good" school were heavily into drug usage, especially the designer drugs such as Ecstasy. That drug contains methamphetamine (Avis 1990), and Debbie told her mother, when she finally confessed her drug usage, "It is so great. You can take it and just dance and dance forever." The amphetamine properties had diet suppression effects, which resulted in the weight loss.

The solution, which we worked out, was to transfer Debbie to one of the "lesser" high schools in the city. We did not know for sure if there was less drug usage there than in the rich kids' school, but at least it got Debbie out of the crowd she was hanging with; her drug use has apparently ceased and her weight is now in her normal range. Oftentimes, a person engages in deviant behavior due to the circumstances in which they find themselves (Eisenman 1991b). Thus, Debbie fell in with a fast crowd of wealthy, upper-class white youth who were into drugs. Of course, deviance can also come about due to the personality of the individual (Eisenman 1991b), and only time will tell if Debbie goes back to drugs.

Conclusions

Debbie's case is consistent with the surprising findings of the National Crime Victimization Survey (Bureau of Justice Statistics 1991c). Drugs may be prevalent in wealthy, white, non-inner city schools, as well as in the more stereotyped inner-city minority schools. Perhaps we should be aware that while drugs are often quite prevalent in the inner-city schools, they are also available in the more wealthy, non-inner-city schools, too. There will be more cases like Debbie, and the national survey has made an important contribution if it makes us more sensitive to this reality.

References

Avis, H. 1990. *Drugs and Life*. Dubuque, IA: William C. Brown.

Bureau of Justice Statistics. 1990a. *The Nation's two crime measures: Uniform Crime Reports and the National Crime Survey*. NCJ–122705, 4/90. Washington, DC: United States Department of Justice.

————. 1990b. *Criminal victimization in the U.S.: 1988*. NCJ–122024, 10/90. Washington, DC: United States Department of Justice.

————. 1991a. *Criminal victimization in the U.S.: 1989*. NCJ–129391, 6/91. Washington, DC: United States Department of Justice.

————. 1991b. *Criminal victimization in the U. S.: 1973–88 trends*. NCJ129392, 7/91. Washington, DC: United States Department of Justice.

————. 1991c. *School crime: A national crime victimization survey report*. By Linda D. Bastian and Bruce M. Taylor, BJS Statisticians, NCJ–131645, 10/91. Washington, DC: United States Department of Justice.

Eisenman, R. 1991a. Conduct disordered youth: Insights from a prison treatment program. *Beyond Behavior*, 2 (1, Winter), 3–4.

————. 1991b. *From crime to creativity: Psychological and social factors in deviance*. Dubuque, IA. Kendall/Hunt.

Associated Press. "Hip-hop generation' still hardest to reach." *Lake Charles American Press*, May 27, 1992, p.18.

MEE Productions. 1992. *Reaching the hip-hop generation*. Philadelphia, PA: Author

---

Author's Note: We thank Bruce M. Taylor, Bureau of Justice Statistics, U. S. Department of Justice, for his assistance.

Who Receives Drug Education in Our Schools? A Paradox

XOX XOX XOX XOX XOX XOX XOX XOX XOX XOX XOX XOX XOX XOX

One of the best approaches to drug prevention would seem to be drug education classes in primary and secondary schools. Such an approach represents primary prevention, where attempts are made to prevent a problem before it happens, as opposed to secondary prevention where a group is targeted after it is already at risk, or tertiary prevention where the treatment occurs after someone has already developed the problem. Unfortunately, most intervention seems to be tertiary: people enter therapy after they are already mentally ill, alcoholic, physically ill, addicted to drugs, etc.

Denson, Voight, and Eisenman (in press) found a paradox regarding AIDS education in Louisiana. Although blacks are at greatest risk for HIV/AIDS, the predominantly black schools reported less AIDS education than the predominantly white schools. This is unfortunate, since those who need the education the most are getting it the least.

The purpose of the present report is to present data from the United States Department of Justice National Crime Victimization Survey (1991) regarding who gets drug education classes in American primary and secondary schools. Drug education seems like an excellent idea, being primary prevention, but it will have limited effectiveness if people who need it do not receive it, as in the Denson et al. (in press) study.

Subjects and Method

The United States Department of Justice conducted the National Crime Victimization Survey, collecting data on crime from a nationally representative sample of 47,000 households in the United States. For the study of school crime, household members between the ages of twelve and nineteen years old were interviewed if they had attended school any time during the preceding six months, and were currently enrolled in a school that would advance them toward the receipt of a high school diploma. This procedure resulted in a sample of 10,449 students. A detailed report of the procedures can be found in another Bureau of Justice Statistics report (1991), especially in appendix III of that report. Students were classified as attending grades six through twelve.

Results

White students were more likely to report receiving drug education classes than were black students, 40% vs. 36%. Students in the central city classrooms were the least likely to receive drug education classes, with 35% reporting receiving such classes vs. 40% in suburban classes and 44% in non-metropolitan areas. Non-metropolitan areas are defined as neither suburban nor near a city, and would thus include rural areas not next to at least a medium size city. While sixth graders were the least likely to believe someone could get drugs at their school, they were the most likely to report receiving drug education classes, 56%; while ninth through twelfth graders were the most likely group to report availability of drugs, but the least likely to receive drug education classes. For ninth graders, 36% reported attending drug education classes, while the percentages were 35% for tenth graders, 33% for eleventh graders, and a low of 27% for twelfth grade students. Looking at drug availability in the schools and whether or not the students attended drug education classes, 44% of the students who said drugs were not available in their school reported attending drug education classes vs. 40% who reported that drugs were available.

Discussion

In every instance reported above, the group that would seem most in need of drug education classes reports being less likely to receive them than groups seemingly less in need of such classes. This is, indeed, a paradox. In part, it could be that drug education classes are effective, so that where they occur, drugs are less available in the schools. This would account for those who report drugs not available in their schools being more likely to report attending drug education classes, relative to those who report drugs are available in their school. However, such an explanation could only account for part of the data. It would not, for example, explain why whites are more likely to receive drug education classes than blacks.

As paradoxical as the data are, they are also consistent with the finding by Denson et al. (in press) that predominantly black schools in Louisiana were less likely to provide HIV/AIDS education than were predominantly white schools. It may be that the white schools had better funding, better teachers, more concerned parents or community, etc. All this is speculation, attempting to explain why blacks, who are more at risk for the HIV/AIDS virus than are whites, would have received less classroom education on the matter. As related to the data of the present study, it may be that blacks, students in central city schools, etc., get the short end of the stick when it comes to education, with greater resources going to the wealthier school districts (Eisenman, unpublished manuscript; Kozol 1991). Thus, there is a perpetuation of poverty and racism if this explanation is correct.

The data is based on self report, and may reflect perceptions rather than realities in some instances. However, the consistency of the findings gives some assurance that a real phenomenon is present. There are policy implications from these findings. We cannot assume that just because someone is at risk for a problem that resources will be directed toward helping that person. Rather, we must make sure that programs—be they drug prevention or something else in another context—are provided where needed. The present findings might also alert us to the possibility that people who most need a service may not be likely to receive it, and thus corrective action is necessary.

References

Bureau of Justice Statistics, School Crime: *A National Crime Victimization Survey Report*, U. S. Department of Justice, NCJ–31645, September 1991.

———. *Criminal Victimization in the U. S.: 1989*. U.S. Department of Justice, NCJ–129391, June 1991.

Denson, D., R. Eisenman, and R. Voight. In press. *Who Is Receiving HIV/AIDS Education in the Schools? Adolescence*.

Eisenman, R. *Race, Sex, and Age: A Nationwide Study of Juvenile Crime*. Unpublished manuscript, McNeese State University.

Kozol, J. 1991. *Savage Inequalities*. Crown, New York.

Adolescent and Young Adult Sex Offenders: Are They Sexually Addicted?

XOX XOX XOX XOX XOX XOX XOX XOX XOX XOX XOX XOX XOX XOX

This article discusses characteristics of adolescent and young adult sex offenders, and compares those characteristics to the sexual addiction cycle described by Carnes (1983). The purpose of this is to see if the incarcerated sex offenders I worked with fit the criteria for sexual addiction. Sandhu (1990) described the work of Carnes (1983, 1989) and the controversial concept of sexual addiction, while in the same issue Duncan (1990) also discussed treatment of sex offenders. However, the controversy comes about because "sexual addiction" is a relatively new concept, and some wonder if it is a valid construct. Perhaps all that is being done is saying that society disapproves of certain sexual behavior, thus making deviants of people who engage in such behavior and labeling them negatively (see Eisenman 1991a for a discussion of how societies tend to do this sort of thing in an irrational fashion).

For almost two years I served as Senior Clinical Psychologist in a prison treatment program. I worked in individual and group therapy with sex offenders, ranging in age from sixteen to twenty-eight years old. Most were still incarcerated when I left the prison job, and we can safely predict that most prisoners incarcerated in this prison system, including the sex offenders, will reoffend (Eisenman 1991a, 1991b). However, if treatment results in only a 15% increase in preventing new offenses, over what would have occurred without treatment, then this is a great contribution to society, as many future potential victims will be spared. If the sex offenders I worked with fit the Carnes (1983) criteria for sexual addiction, then it would add to the validity of the concept. If, however, they are notably different, then the "sex addiction" concept would not receive support, and should perhaps be questioned since these sex offenders were repeat, compulsive sex predators. If they are not sex addicts, one might wonder about the usefulness of the sex addict concept. Sandhu (1990) used Carnes' (1983, 1989) sex addict concept to describe sexual issues in the mid-life crisis. Does the sex addict concept also apply to adolescent and young adult sex offenders seen in a prison treatment program?

Addiction Cycle

As Sandhu (1990) pointed out, Carnes (1983) identified four steps of the sexual addiction cycle. I will describe my sex offender patients in terms of these four steps to see it they fit the Carnes sex addict description.

Preoccupation

A sex addict's mind is said to be preoccupied with sexual thoughts and fantasies. While everyone or almost everyone may have sexual thoughts and fantasies, often to what seems like a great extent, the sex addict is even more preoccupied with sexual thoughts, such that they play an overly-important part in his/her life. Obviously, value judgments are being made here. What is the standard for saying that something is overly-important? However, in the extreme case, there may not be any room for dispute. For the sex offenders I worked with, it seems clear that sexual preoccupation was a major facet of their lives. They constantly thought about sex, often of a kind disapproved of by society, such as molesting children or raping women. Their conscious thoughts, fantasies, and masturbation fantasies and behavior were frequent and sexually directed. Sex seemed to play a disproportionate part in their lives, both including thoughts and actual behavior. So this first part of the sex addiction cycle supports Carnes (1983), in that the sex offenders were preoccupied with sex, as Carnes might be expected to predict.

Ritualization

Here we have a concept which is open to criticism. Carnes (1983) says that the ritualizations intensify the excitement of the sex addict, and discusses the ritualized behavior, such as cruising back and forth in the same area while trying to pick up sexual partners. My criticism would be that normal, non-addicted people engage in what could be called rituals. The whole dating pattern of our society is a ritual. People go through courtship rituals when they interact with each other in romantic situations. Much of everyday life is ritual: "How are you?" "Fine, how are you?" This everyday ritual has nothing to do with getting information on how one is, but with showing that you acknowledge the other's existence in a friendly fashion, and they reciprocate. All this said, it follows that the sex offenders in the prison I worked in did engage in ritualized behaviors. They learned that certain behaviors worked to victimize others, and they stuck with these behaviors, such as the child molester enticing little children by offering them candy. Once this has been successful, the child molester stalks the playgrounds or parks searching for potential victims and using the same lines on them: "Hi. Would you like some candy?" While this seems to support Carnes, is it any different than the stereotyped fashion in which men and women in our society talk to each other when they are attracted, e.g., "Hi. What are you reading?" Support for the sex addict concept here is, then, tentative, since the whole ritualization concept might be too general to be useful. Perhaps what would be useful would be a study of the specific "rituals," which sex offenders use, in order to warn potential victims.

Compulsive sexual behavior

Addicts are said to be powerless in controlling their sexual behavior. They seem driven. Here, the sex offenders once again supported the concept of sexual addiction, as they seemed driven in what they were doing. It was unimaginable to them that they might cease their sexual behavior, even though it was highly antisocial, hurt others, and could get them in great trouble. This is, in part, why recidivism rates for sex offenders are so high (Eisenman 1991a, 1991b; French 1991; Rice, Quinsey, and Harris 1991). Compulsive behaviors are difficult to stop, even when people realize that it is in their best interest to cease the conduct. In this sense, sexual addiction seems at least analogous to drug addiction, with both being things people cannot control.

Despair

In the fourth stage of the sexual addiction cycle, people feel terrible about their sexual behavior. They are ashamed, embarrassed, and wish it had never happened. While all three of the stages above fit the sex offenders I worked with, this fourth stage clearly does not. They appeared quite happy with their sexual victimization of others, and the only regrets they had was being captured and imprisoned. I would suggest that it is only through therapy that many sex offenders come to see that there is anything wrong with what they have done. This may seem amazing in light of the great antisocial nature of their behavior, but they do not have the same kind of conscience that normal people have, at least not with regard to sexual behavior. Something to be guarded against is that sex offenders are often very crafty, and if they figure out that the way to win their freedom is to say that they have remorse, then they will say it. However, what the therapist wants is true remorse, not simple verbal parroting of what the therapist wants to hear.

Case Histories

Two case histories of young sex offenders are presented, which show what sex offenders can be like, and illustrate some of the problems as well as potential therapeutic benefits in working with sex offenders. In both cases, I worked with the offender in individual and group psychotherapy for about one year, and each received group therapy treatment from other therapists within the prison treatment, setting.

Jack

The prisoner I shall call Jack was a sixteen-year old, white youth who was extremely effeminate. As if this was not bad enough for his welfare in a prison, where toughness and macho standards prevail among the inmates (and guards, too), the fact that he was a sex offender added to his travail. Sex offenders are typically hated by other prisoners, who use them as scapegoats, saying, "As bad as I am, I would never do something like that." Further, instead of trying to conceal his crimes, when Jack first entered our prison he often boasted, "I sodomized a nine-year old, and I am proud of it." This earned him great hatred from the other prisoners.

Why would Jack boast of the offense that sent him to prison? In therapy it became apparent that it went back to the time when he was nine-years old and his father, a homosexual or bisexual, made him wear a dress and anally raped him on several occasions. I never knew the father, as he committed suicide several years earlier, but I suspect he was effeminate and that Jack modeled himself after the father.

Jack was placed in a boys' home when his mother went to jail for credit card fraud. Thus, he had a dead father and a criminal mother. Jack also revealed things in therapy, which suggested that his mother was a prostitute, although he never came out and said it directly. He did say, "She worked at an X-rated motel and had sex with eighty-six men in one year." I spoke with his mother on the phone about release plans for Jack, and she seemed like a normal, charming person, which of course would be helpful if one is a prostitute or doing credit card forgery. Jack was serving a four-year sentence, and the Youthful Offender Parole Board made it clear that they would have him serve all four years, with no early parole, which is unusual. Typically, prisoners are considered for parole before their full sentence expires.

As is typical with sex offenders, Jack had many more victims than the one he was convicted for (Eisenman 1991a, 1991b). He is a physically weak, obese youth with pimples all over his face and the top of his head. His hygiene habits are poor. He seems to not have brushed his teeth or combed his hair on any regular basis. Besides the modeling after a homosexual rapist father, Jack seemed motivated to commit the sex offenses as a way of establishing power. He is a bully to boys weaker than him although most of the time he is bullied by stronger kids. While most bullies choose physical combat and intimidation, Jack's background led him to utilize sex.

I met with Jack in individual therapy sessions at least twice a week and we established a good therapeutic relationship. I also went beyond the usual call of duty and tried to insure his physical safety from other prisoners, by talking to guards who took him to recreation and other group activities, and asking them to watch out for attack against Jack.

Jack refused to go to the prison swimming pool, fearing the rough play which the prisoners engaged in, such as dunking each other. Also, this would have been an opportune time for someone to really hurt him, such as attempted drowning, so he probably displayed good judgment in refusing to go to the pool. As with many of the prisoners, I, as a therapist, was one of the few people who had ever shown interest in Jack or treated him with dignity. Most of the prisoners came from tragic back grounds of poverty and neglect.

Will Jack reoffend when he gets out? No one can say. The therapy sessions (including others set up in our prison treatment program such as sex offenders group therapy) seemed to have helped him learn that molesting kids is wrong. At one point in therapy, after many sessions, he said, "I should die for what I did to Benny" (his victim). This is an improvement over being proud of the offense. On the other hand, he is returning to a criminal mother who no doubt neglected him in the past. It would not make sense to send him back to the state boys' home where his offenses occurred, and the mother may be the best that can be done. From studying the records of our prisoners and talking with them, foster homes are often terrible places, where more neglect occurs. So, while I would not want to bet any money on Jack's chances, I suspect they are much better than when he had no treatment.

Roy

I have briefly discussed some things about Roy previously (Eisenman 1990), since he is so interesting. An 18-year old black youth, Roy was in prison for two robberies, one in which he and fellow Crip gang members (a notorious black youth gang, famous for much antisocial behavior including cocaine sales and drive-by killings) took jewelry from a jewelry store by grabbing it and trying to run out. They assaulted a security guard who tried to stop them. Roy admits this crime, but denied his other conviction, a robbery of two elderly women who were allegedly hit and robbed by Roy as they started to enter their car. Like Jack, he was on my individual therapy caseload, and was seen by me in various therapy groups. Unlike Jack, Roy was not identified as a sex offender, and was not required to attend the sex offender's therapy group. This was unfortunate, since he showed many characteristics of a sex offender, although he had not been convicted for any sex crime nor was his former male prostitution widely known to staff. He spoke to me in individual therapy of how he had, several years ago, worn a miniskirt and been a homosexual prostitute.

In addition, Roy was an incredibly angry person, and threatened at least two of the female staff members with rape. This did not seem to be an idle threat, as one of his favorite ploys was to wait until female staff passed by the window of his room and to masturbate in a way that they could see him. Thus, he used sex in a passive-aggressive fashion, with the potential of being a rapist to express his anger, which was especially strong against women. Roy saw his mother die when he was four years old, and perhaps this has contributed to a perception of women as being people who abandon you. He has been abandoned and rejected much of his life, although most of it seems to have been by men. His birth father abandoned the family before Roy was born, and as a child he was raped by an uncle. Thus, like Jack, the genesis of his sexual offending seems to stem, in part, from being sexually abused, himself. All or almost all of our sex offenders had, themselves, been sexually abused in their early years. Thus, they had been victims, and were now victimizing others.

On another occasion, Roy was missing from the classroom. The teacher searched the staff restroom and she found Roy in there, masturbating. Possibly he was planning to rape her. As he would often do, he denied he was doing anything wrong, and said he only went in there to use the bathroom. At times, he would be amazingly honest with me in therapy, and tell me things that could be damaging to him, such as misdeeds he had either not been caught doing, or had been accused of but with insufficient evidence to prove his misconduct. At other times, he would blatantly lie to me. At first, I thought that since he was so honest with me about things, that when he denied something he must be telling the truth, but later I learned that this was not the case.

In both individual and group psychotherapy, Roy revealed to me some frightening fantasies. In his mind these are not fantasies, but plans. He said that he has a list of fifty-six people he intends to kill when he gets out. He is scheduled for release in a few years. Also, he wants to go to a shopping mall with an Uzi submachine gun and randomly kill people. If he is successful at the first mall, then he wants to go to a second and repeat the behavior. He assumes he would be killed at the second mall, if not at the first. This second fantasy or plan is consistent with the suicidal qualities he shows at times. On occasion, he burns his skin with matches; although this is, of course, against the prison rules.

Roy feels he has been victimized his entire life, and in some ways this is an accurate assessment. The one stable home he had was a group home run by a black woman, which included white as well as black youths. A social worker concluded that Roy "was not getting the black experience" there, and had him removed after about four years in this stable setting. Then began a succession of placements, including one with the uncle who raped him; unfortunately, all ended in rejection and new, unsuccessful placements. This is an example of how one's political views may not be in the best interest of the client. What that social worker did was, in my opinion, inexcusable, and I feel that the social worker has on his or her hands (I do not know who the social worker was, but I have verified the story), the blood of Roy's future victims.

Conclusions

Adolescent and young adult sex offenders seen in a prison treatment program fit three of the four stages of the sexual addiction cycle, as described by Carnes (1983) and summarized by Sandhu (1990). However, one of the stages, ritualization, is perhaps too general to have much meaning. Both Jack and Roy, discussed in the case histories above, were preoccupied with their sexual deviance and were compulsive in carrying out their sexual fantasies of molesting children (Jack) or using sex in a passive-aggressive fashion (Roy's masturbation in view of female staff). Neither seemed able or willing to stop what they were doing. The sex offenders in the prison clearly did not fit stage four, despair. They had no remorse and were perhaps lacking in conscience development in the sexual area, if not other areas as well. It seems that the Carnes (1983, 1989) description of sexual addiction has some usefulness in describing the adolescent or young adult sex offender, but is inaccurate with regard to the issue of despair, since the sex offenders I worked with showed no remorse except as a result of treatment, and even here one has to be careful about being manipulated by devious offenders seeking freedom.

Future research should be done on how people become sex offenders, and how different life experiences or personality makeup may be related to different kinds of sexual offense. For example, there may be important differences between child molesters and rapists. Both are sex offenders, but they have chosen different ways of offending, and may have some fundamental differences, as well as similarities. Another important area is how to make offenders remorseful in a lasting fashion. Some may be remorseful for a brief period of time, if they are not lying to the therapist, but I fear this may not last. How can we achieve a lasting change? A related research need is to discover how to install a conscience, or at least a better conscience, in these people. Can we overcome the early years of abuse they suffered and get them to have true empathy for others? Or, is it too late, even by the time someone is sixteen years old? This is a very important question, and what we do with sex offenders would vary greatly depending upon whether or not we can effect change in them. I suspect that therapists who have not worked with sex offenders, or who have not worked in a prison, would be more optimistic than those who have worked with hard core sex offenders of the type found in a prison setting. Prison therapists are often disillusioned and pessimistic. Whose view of reality is more correct? My final suggestion is that we have rigorous follow up of sex offenders, both to continue treatment once they leave the prison or the therapist's office, and to see which treatments have the most effect. For instance, in a given type of case, is treatment in a prison setting better or worse than outpatient treatment in reducing sexual offenses? These and many other issues are necessary for learning how to deal with sex offenders and making their lives better and protecting potential future victims.

References

Carnes, P. 1983. *Out of the shadows: Understanding sexual addiction.* Minneapolis, MN: CompCare Publishers.

———. 1989. *Contrary to love: Helping the sexual addict.* Minneapolis, MN: CompCare Publishers.

Duncan, B. B. 1990. Sexual offender treatment option program. *Journal of Young Adulthood and Middle Age, 2,* 97–112.

Eisenman, R. 1990. Six problems of a prison psychologist: A personal account. *Psychological Reports, 67,* 755–761.

———. 1991a. *From crime to creativity: Psychological and social factors in deviance.* Dubuque, IA: Kendall/Hunt.

———. 1991b. Monitoring and post confinement treatment of sex offenders: An urgent need. *Psychological Reports, 69,* 1089–1090.

French, L. 1991. A practitioner's notes on treating sexual deviance. *Psychological Reports, 68,* 1195–1198.

Rice, M. E., G. Harris, and V. L. Quinsey. 1991. Sexual recidivism among child molesters released from a maximum security psychiatric institution. *Journal of Consulting and Clinical Psychology, 59,* 381–386.

Sandhu, D. S. 1990. Resolution of mid-life crisis: The sexually addicted. *Journal of Young Adulthood and Middle Age, 2,* 89–96.

Belief That Drug Usage in the United States Is Increasing When It Is Really Decreasing

An Example of the Availability Heuristic

XOX XOX XOX XOX XOX XOX XOX XOX XOX XOX XOX XOX XOX XOX

According to Tversky and Kahneman (1974) people often use shorthand methods for understanding the world. These heuristics include the availability heuristic, where probability of events is judged on how readily they come to mind; and the representativeness heuristic, where an event or object is seen as belonging to a category the more closely it resembles the typical instance. With regard to the availability heuristic, distorted perceptions could occur because an event is emphasized in the mass media. Taylor and Cook (1984) found evidence for this kind of distortion due to media emphasis. A current media emphasis is on drugs. The United States has a "War on Drugs" and the media often reports about people arrested for drug possession or sales. Some newspapers carry daily stories of drug arrests, while there are several television shows known as "reality programming" in which real-life drug raids are shown. In one such reality program, *American Detectives*, almost every show is about drug raids, as opposed to, say, detectives investigating burglaries or murders.

Based on the above, it may be that if people were asked to judge if drug usage in the United States is increasing or decreasing, they would definitely be inclined to see it as increasing, whether or not this is actually the case. The constant emphasis by the mass media, and the actual frequency of arrests due to the "War on Drugs," would make people think that drug usage is increasing out of control, and just keeps getting worse and worse. If drug usage is not increasing, then we would have the operation of the availability heuristic (Tversky and Kahneman 1974). However, we need to know what the actual amount of drug usage in the United States really is, and has been in past years. Fortunately, there are impressive data available from nationwide household surveys conducted by the National Commission on Marijuana and Drug Abuse, and sponsored by the National Institute on Drug Abuse. These samples of data from 1972–1990 can be compared with what students think is the case about whether drug usage in the United States is increasing or decreasing.

Method

Subjects

The participants were 104 undergraduate college students at a state university, from two introduction to psychology classes, who participated during their classes. The data on actual drug usage was obtained from the National Household Survey on Drug Abuse, and involved 9,259 respondents in households in the contiguous United States.

Procedure

In the college classrooms, students were asked, "Is drug usage in the United States increasing or decreasing over the past several years?" They were urged to write down one of the two alternatives on their sheet of paper, but in response to a small number of questions, they were told that it was permissible to write "don't know" or "staying the same." Four subjects gave this kind of answer, and their data was not used. In past studies by the author, the vast majority of students do not choose the intermediate categories, except when it is something they feel ignorant about.

For the National Household Survey on Drug Abuse, begun in 1971 under the auspices of the National Commission on Marijuana and Drug Abuse and sponsored by the National Institute on Drug Abuse, 9,259 respondents were asked about their usage of both legal and illegal drugs. The survey sampled people twelve years of age and older living in households in the contiguous United States. Personal interviews and self-administered answer sheets were used. To find out about drug usage, the following groups were purposely oversampled: blacks, Hispanics, young people, and residents of the metropolitan Washington, DC area. Otherwise, the sampling was done to be representative of people living in households in the United States (with the exception of Alaska and Hawaii). Omitted from this survey of households was the homeless; people living in military installations, dormitories or other group quarters; and, those in institutions such as hospitals or jails.

Results

For the college students, seventy said that drug usage is increasing, and thirty reported that drug usage is decreasing $\chi^2(1) = 16,$ $<p$ .001, two-tailed test). None gave intermediate answers such as "neither increasing nor decreasing," "staying the same," nor did any answer "don't know."

In comparison with the college students' belief that drug usage is increasing, the data from tables 8.1–8.3 show that drug usage, for both legal and illegal drugs, has been decreasing in recent years. Table 8.1 reports the data in terms of lifetime prevalence of drug usage, i.e., has the person ever used the drug? Table 8.2 reports the data in terms of annual drug usage, i.e., usage within the past year, while table 8.3 reports the data in terms of usage within the past month. All three tables get at drug usage by the subject, but each covers a different time period. Thus, if a person used a drug ten years ago but not since, it would show up in table 8.1, Lifetime Prevalence, but not in tables 8.2 or 8.3.

Although drug usage has been decreasing in recent years, according to the survey data, there are still many millions of Americans who use drugs, as shown in table 8.4. Thus, "decreasing" does not mean anything like "nonexistent."

Table 8.1
Lifetime Prevalence of Drug Use: 1972 to 1990

	Youth age 12–17								
	1972	1974	1976	1977	1979	1982	1985	1988	1990
Marijuana	14.0%	23.0%	22.4%	28.0%	30.9%	26.7%	23.6%	17.4%	14.89%
Hallucinogens	4.8	6.0	5.1	4.6	7.1	5.2	3.3	3.5	3.3
Cocaine	1.5	3.6	3.4	4.0	5.4	6.5	4.9	3.4	2.6
Heroin	0.6	1.0	0.5	1.1	0.5	*	*	0.6	0.7
Nonmedical Use of:									
Stimulants	4.0	5.0	4.4	5.2	3.4	6.7	5.6	4.2	4.5
Sedatives	3.0	5.0	2.8	3.1	3.2	5.8	4.1	2.4	3.3
Tranquilizers	3.0	3.0	3.3	3.8	4.1	4.9	4.8	2.0	2.7
Analgesics	-	-	-	-	3.2	4.2	5.8	4.2	6.5
Alcohol	-	54.0	53.6	52.6	70.3	65.2	55.5	50.2	48.2
Cigarettes	-	52.0	45.5	47.3	54.1	49.5	45.2	42.3	40.2
Any Illicit Use	-	-	-	-	34.4	27.6	29.5	24.7	22.7
	Young Adults age 18–25								
	1972	1974	1976	1977	1979	1982	1985	1988	1990
Marijuana	47.9%	52.7%	52.9%	59.9%	68.2%	64.1%	60.3%	56.4%	52.2%
Hallucinogens	-	16.6	17.3	19.8	25.1	21.1	11.3	13.8	12.0
Cocaine	9.1	12.7	13.4	19.1	27.5	28.3	25.2	19.7	19.4
Heroin	4.6	4.5	3.9	3.6	3.5	1.2	1.2	0.4	0.6

(Table 8.1 continued)

Nonmedical Use of:	1972	1974	1976	1977	1979	1982	1985	1988	1990
Stimulants	12.0	17.0	16.6	21.2	18.2	18.0	17.1	11.3	9.0
Sedatives	10.0	15.0	11.9	18.4	17.0	18.7	11.0	5.5	4.0
Tranquilizers	7.0	10.0	9.1	13.4	15.8	15.1	12.0	7.8	5.9
Analgesics	-	-	-	-	11.8	12.1	11.3	9.4	8.1
Alcohol	-	81.6	83.6	84.2	95.3	94.6	92.6	90.3	88.2
Cigarettes	-	68.8	70.1	67.6	82.8	76.9	75.6	75.0	70.5
Any Illicit Use	-	-	-	-	69.9	65.3	64.3	58.9	55.8

Older Adults age 26 +

	1972	1974	1976	1977	1979	1982	1985	1988	1990
Marijuana	7.4%	9.9%	12.9%	15.3%	19.6%	23.0%	27.2%	30.7%	31.8%
Hallucinogens	-	1.3	1.6	2.6	4.5	6.4	6.2	6.6	7.4
Cocaine	1.6	0.9	1.6	2.6	4.3	8.5	9.5	9.9	10.9
Heroin	*	0.5	0.5	0.8	1.0	1.1	1.1	1.1	0.9
Nonmedical Use of:									
Stimulants	3.0	3.0	5.6	4.7	5.8	6.2	7.9	6.6	6.9
Sedatives	2.0	2.0	2.4	2.8	3.5	4.8	5.2	3.3	3.7
Tranquilizers	5.0	2.0	2.7	2.6	3.1	3.6	7.2	4.6	4.2
Analgesics	-	-	-	-	2.7	3.2	5.6	4.5	5.1
Alcohol	-	73.2	74.7	77.9	91.5	88.2	89.4	88.6	86.8
Cigarettes	-	65.4	64.5	67.0	83.0	78.7	80.5	79.6	78.0
Any Illicit Use	-	-	-	-	23.0	24.7	31.5	33.7	35.3

-Estimate not available
*Low precision—no estimate shown

Table 8.2
Annual Drug Use: 1972 to 1990

	1972	1974	1976	1977	1979	1982	1985	1988	1990
			Youth age 12–17						
Marijuana	-	18.5%	18.4%	22.3%	24.1%	20.6%	19.7%	12.6%	11.3
Hallucinogens	3.6	4.3	2.8	3.1	4.7	3.6	2.7	2.8	2.4
Cocaine	1.5	2.7	2.3	2.6	4.2	4.1	4.0	2.9	2.2
Heroin	*	*	*	0.6	*	*	*	0.4	0.6
Nonmedical Use of:									
Stimulants	-	3.0	2.2	3.7	2.9	5.6	4.3	2.8	3.0
Sedatives	-	2.0	1.2	2.0	2.2	3.7	2.9	1.7	2.2
Tranquilizers	-	2.0	1.8	2.9	2.7	3.3	3.4	1.6	1.5
Analgesics	-	-	-	-	2.2	3.7	3.8	3.0	4.8
Alcohol	-	51.0	49.3	47.5	53.6	52.4	51.7	44.6	41.0
Cigarettes	-	-	-	-	13.3**	24.8	25.8	22.8	22.2
Any Illicit Use	-	-	-	-	26.0	22.0	23.7	16.8	15.9
	1972	1974	1976	1977	1979	1982	1985	1988	1990
			Young Adults age 18–25						
Marijuana	-	34.2%	35.0%	38.7%	46.9%	40.4%	36.9%	27.9%	24.6
Hallucinogens	-	6.1	6.0	6.4	9.9	6.9	4.0	5.6	3.9
Cocaine	-	8.1	7.0	10.2	19.6	18.8	16.3	12.1	7.5
Heroin	-	0.8	0.6	1.2	0.8	*	0.6	0.3	0.5

(Table 8.2 continued)

Nonmedical Use of:	1972	1974	1976	1977	1979	1982	1985	1988	1990
Stimulants	-	8.0	8.8	10.4	10.1	10.8	9.9	6.4	3.4
Sedatives	-	4.2	5.7	8.2	7.3	8.7	5.0	3.3	2.0
Tranquilizers	-	4.6	6.2	7.8	7.1	5.9	6.4	4.6	2.4
Analgesics	-	-	-	-	5.2	4.4	6.6	5.5	4.1
Alcohol	-	77.1	77.9	79.8	86.6	87.1	87.2	81.7	80.2
Cigarettes	-	-	-	-	46.7**	47.2	44.3	44.7	39.7
Any Illicit Use	-	-	-	-	49.4	43.4	42.6	32.0	28.7

Older Adults age 26+	1972	1974	1976	1977	1979	1982	1985	1988	1990
Marijuana	-	3.8%	5.4%	6.4%	9.0%	10.6%	9.5%	6.9%	7.3
Hallucinogens	-	*	*	*	0.5	0.8	1.0	0.6	0.4
Cocaine	-	*	0.6	0.9	2.0	3.8	4.2	2.7	2.4
Heroin	-	*	*	*	*	*	*	0.3	0.1
Nonmedical Use of:									
Stimulants	-	*	0.8	0.8	1.3	1.7	2.6	1.7	1.0
Sedatives	-	*	0.6	*	0.8	1.4	2.0	1.2	0.8
Tranquilizers	-	*	1.2	1.1	0.9	1.1	2.8	1.8	1.0
Analgesics	-	-	-	-	0.5	1.0	2.9	2.1	1.9
Alcohol	-	62.7	64.2	65.8	72.4	72.0	73.6	68.6	66.6
Cigarettes	-	-	-	-	39.7**	38.2	36.0	33.7	31.9
Any Illicit Use	-	-	-	-	10.0	11.8	13.3	10.2	10.0

-Estimate not available
* Low precision--no estimate shown
**Includes only persons who ever smoked at least 5 packs

Table 8.3
Current (past month) Drug Use: 1972 to 1990

Youth age 12–17

	1972	1974	1976	1977	1979	1982	1985	1988	1990
Marijuana	7.0%	12.0%	12.3%	16.6%	16.7%	11.5%	12.0%	6.4%	5.2%
Hallucinogens	1.4	1.3	0.9	1.6	2.2	1.4	1.2	0.8	0.9
Cocaine	0.6	1.0	1.0	0.8	1.4	1.6	1.5	1.1	0.6
Heroin	*	*	*	*	*	*	*	*	*
Nonmedical Use of:									
Stimulants	-	1.0	1.2	1.3	1.2	2.6	1.6	1.2	1.0
Sedatives	-	1.0	*	0.8	1.1	1.3	1.0	0.6	0.9
Tranquilizers	-	1.0	1.1	0.7	0.6	0.9	0.6	0.2	0.5
Analgesics	-	-	-	-	0.6	0.7	1.6	0.9	1.4
Alcohol	-	34.0	32.4	31.2	37.2	30.2	31.0	25.2	24.5
Cigarettes	-	25.0	23.4	22.3	12.1**	14.7	15.3	11.8	11.6
Any Illicit Use	-	-	-	-	17.6	12.7	14.9	9.2	8.1

Young Adults age 18–25

	1972	1974	1976	1977	1979	1982	1985	1988	1990
Marijuana	27.8%	25.2%	25.0%	27.4%	35.4%	27.4%	21.8%	15.5%	12.7%
Hallucinogens	-	2.5	1.1	2.0	4.4	1.7	1.9	1.9	0.8
Cocaine	-	3.1	2.0	3.7	9.3	6.8	7.6	4.5	2.2
Heroin	-	*	*	*	*	*	*	*	*

(Table 8.3 continued)

Nonmedical Use of:

	1972	1974	1976	1977	1979	1982	1985	1988	1990
Stimulants	-	3.7	4.7	2.5	3.5	4.7	3.7	2.4	1.2
Sedatives	-	1.6	2.3	2.8	2.8	2.6	1.6	0.9	0.7
Tranquilizers	-	1.2	2.6	2.4	2.1	1.6	1.6	1.0	0.5
Analgesics	-	-	-	-	1.0	1.0	1.8	1.5	1.2
Alcohol	-	69.3	69.0	70.0	75.9	70.9	71.4	65.3	63.3
Cigarettes	-	48.4	49.4	47.3	42.6**	39.5	36.8	35.2	31.5
Any Illicit Use	-	-	-	-	37.1	30.4	25.7	17.8	14.9

Older Adults age 26+

	1972	1974	1976	1977	1979	1982	1985	1988	1990
Marijuana	2.5%	2.0%	3.5%	3.3%	6.0%	6.6%	6.1%	3.9%	3.6%
Hallucinogens	-	*	*	*	*	*	*	*	0.1
Cocaine	-	*	*	*	0.9	1.2	2.0	0.9	0.6
Heroin	-	*	*	*	*	*	*	*	*
Nonmedical Use of:									
Stimulants	-	*	*	0.6	0.5	0.6	0.7	0.5	0.3
Sedatives	-	*	0.5	*	*	*	0.6	0.3	0.1
Tranquilizers	-	*	*	*	*	*	1.0	0.6	0.2
Analgesics	-	-	-	-	*	*	0.9	0.4	0.6
Alcohol	-	54.5	56.0	54.9	61.3	59.8	60.6	54.8	52.3
Cigarettes	-	39.1	38.4	38.7	36.9**	34.6	32.8	29.8	27.7
Any Illicit Use	-	-	-	-	6.5	7.5	8.5	4.9	4.6

-Estimate not available
* Low precision—no estimate shown
**Includes only persons who ever smoked at least 5 packs

Table 8.4
Population Estimates of Lifetime and Current Drug Use, 1990

The following are estimates of the number of people twelve years of age and older who report they have used drugs nonmedically. Drugs used under a physician's care are not included. The estimates were developed from the 1990 National Household Survey on Drug Abuse.

	12-17 yrs. (pop. 19,977,918)				18-25yrs. (pop. 29,020,582)			
	%	Ever Used	%	Current User	%	Ever Used	%	Current User
Marijuana and Hashish	15	2,954,000	5	1,030,000	52	15,140,000	13	3,692,000
Hallucinogens	3	652,000	1	186,000	12	3,485,000	1	243,000
Inhalants	8	1,548,000	2	441,000	10	3,019,000	1	344,000
Cocaine	3	518,000	1	115,000	19	5,620,000	2	630,000
Crack	1	201,000	*	45,000	3	802,000	1	192,000
Heroin	1	145,000	*	7,000	1	166,000	*	25,000
Stimulants	5	898,000	1	191,000	9	2,621,000	1	350,000
Sedatives	3	658,000	1	182,000	4	1,157,000	1	215,000
Tranquilizers	3	533,000	1	110,000	6	1,702,000	1	151,000
Analgesics	7	1,292,000	1	274,000	8	2,349,000	1	340,000
Alcohol	48	9,636,000	25	4,895,000	88	25,599,000	63	18,368,000
Cigarettes	40	8,041,000	12	2,327,000	71	20,468,000	32	9,143,000
Smokeless Tobacco	12	2,356,000	4	775,000	22	6,306,000	6	1,734,000

(Table 8.4 continued)

	26+ yrs. (pop. 152,189,483)				TOTAL (pop. 201,187,983)			
	%	Ever Used	%	Current User	%	Ever Used	%	Current User
Marijuana and Hashish	32	48,413,000	4	5,483,000	33	66,507,000	6	10,206,000
Hallucinogens	7	11,203,000	*	*	8	15,339,000	*	553,000
Inhalants	4	5,729,000	*	*	5	10,296,000	1	1,188,000
Cocaine	11	16,601,000	1	856,000	11	22,739,000	1	1,601,000
Crack	1	1,755,000	*	*	1	2,757,000	*	494,000
Heroin	1	1,343,000	*	*	1	1,654,000	*	48,000
Stimulants	7	10,444,000	*	*	7	13,963,000	1	957,000
Sedatives	4	5,700,000	*	*	4	7,515,000	*	568,000
Tranquilizers	4	6,433,000	*	*	4	8,668,000	*	568,000
Analgesics	5	7,766,000	1	923,000	6	11,408,000	1	1,536,000
Alcohol	87	132,145,000	52	79,656,000	83	167,380,000	51	102,919,000
Cigarettes	78	118,733,000	28	42,162,000	73	147,241,000	27	53,633,000
Smokeless Tobacco	13	19,710,000	3	4,602,000	14	28,372,000	4	7,111,000

*Amounts of less than 5% are not listed.
Terms:
Ever Used: used at least once in a person's lifetime.
Current User: used at least once in the 30 days prior to the survey.

Discussion

The students would seem to have been the victims of the availability heuristic. Since there is so much in the mass media about drug usage, the students judge that drug usage must be increasing. Mass media can, at times, result in people misperceiving things (Tyler and Cook 1984), as well as, at other times, informing people correctly. Since acts may be judged negatively due to the perception of their social importance (Eisenman 1991), the misjudgments due to heuristics can influence whether or not a person or a group is judged as acceptable or unacceptable. Note that these judgments may be based on faulty reasoning, e.g., if a marijuana smoker is judged as just as dangerous to society as a cocaine user, due to the media reporting sensationalistic stories about each. Or, if a person who belongs to a minority political party is judged as being like a Communist, because the person doing the judging has faulty reasoning about these concepts. Thus, heuristics can lead to judgments of deviance and the ensuing hatred (Eisenman 1991).

This article assumes that the government data is correct and that the student judgments are incorrect. Is it possible it could be the other way around? While it seems unlikely, it should be considered that the students may have access to data the government surveys do not reveal. For example, the students may know, from personal experience, that use of drugs is increasing, while respondents to the government survey may give dishonest answers. In this scenario, the students would be correct, and the results would be explained without using the heuristics concept.

It would be possible to ask the students about drug usage in more detailed fashion. For example, they could be asked about specific drugs, such as having a questionnaire which mentions each drug and has the student rate "increasing" or "decreasing." Or, the students could be asked to rate the increasing-decreasing information on a 1-to-7 scale, so that intermediate answers would not be discouraged. Also, it might be useful to counterbalance the order of the questions used in the present study, so that some subjects are asked first about drug usage decreasing, then asked about drug usage increasing, to control for possible order effects.

The study seems to show the operation of the availability heuristic (Tversky and Hahneman 1974). Students think drug usage has been increasing, while nationwide surveys suggest that in recent years drug usage is decreasing. The mass media would seem to be the likely basis of this student misperception, but educational classes on drug abuse and the frequent comments by people in authority might also contribute. Also, as table 8.4 showed, drug usage is widespread in the United States, and this may influence the students' perceptions. It might be difficult to think that something so widespread is, at the same time, decreasing in frequency.

References

Eisenman, R. 1991. *From crime to creativity: Psychological and social factors in deviance.* Dubuque, IA: Kendall/Hunt.

Tversky, A., and D. Kahneman. 1974. Judgment under uncertainty: Heuristics and biases. *Science, 185,* 1124–113 1.

Tyler, T. R., and F .L. Cook. 1984. The mass media and judgments of risk: Distinguishing impact on personal and societal level judgments. *Journal of Personality and Social Psychology, 47,* 693–708.

Mistreatment of the Mentally Ill in a Prison Treatment Program

XOX XOX XOX XOX XOX XOX XOX XOX XOX XOX XOX XOX XOX XOX

This article describes my observations of the nearly two years that I served as Senior Clinical Psychologist in a prison treatment program for youthful male offenders, operated by the state of California. I have described certain aspects elsewhere (Eisenman 1990, 1991b, 1992). There were forty-three beds for prisoners in the treatment program, and an additional five beds for treatment of acutely suicidal prisoners. These beds were located in small rooms in which the prisoners were confined. Thus, the prison had rooms rather than cells, but except for the psychotherapy, it was clearly a prison environment. I refer to "prisoners," but they were called "wards," as in "wards of the court." However, I believe that prisoner is a better word to describe them, and is a term better understood by readers not connected with this particular prison system. People whom I would call guards (and will refer to as "guards" in this article, except when I mention their title) were called Youth Counselors, although they carried handcuffs and mace, and did little counseling. Their responsibilities were largely security, although they did not wear correctional officer uniforms, like the other security staff, but wore their own clothes.

The prisoners received much individual and group psychotherapy in an effort to change them. About one-third of the forty-three prisoners were psychotic. The others all had to be considered emotionally disturbed to get into the program. Thus, the program was designed to give treatment and some compassion to those prisoners with emotional problems. The program had originally been designed for psychotic prisoners admitted into the California Youth Authority system from Los Angeles County. But it had been expanded to be the prison treatment program for the Youth Authority for all of Southern

California and parts of central California. There are only two other treatment programs in the Youth Authority, both in northern California, and both with forty-three beds. Thus, only the most emotionally disturbed of the approximately 8,000 youth in the California Youth Authority prison system get to go to a treatment program. To be sentenced to the California Youth Authority, a person has to be under twenty-five years of age and to have either (a) a long history of crime or (b) to have committed a very serious offense, such as kidnapping, rape, or murder. Most fit category (a) although about five were typically not long-term criminals but were committed as a result of committing perhaps one serious crime.

As an insider, I got to see how things were actually done. Prisons tend to be very secretive places, and outsiders are prevented from learning what really occurs. In part, this is because staff can lose their jobs in political shakeups if there is bad publicity. Thus, there is reinforcement for being secretive. Even insiders do not always get to know what is going on, due to the secretive nature of the prison institution. For example, I could not say how many prisoners were raped while I was there. The few instances I knew about, I heard of almost by chance. This kind of thing was not widely publicized, even within the prison, even to therapists. Three kinds of coercion are reported here. The first two seem clearly wrong and constitute physical and/or psychological abuse. The third one seems proper to me, and could be utilized in other institutions which work with offenders, or by psychotherapists who are engaged in treating criminals.

Shackled to a Marble Slab in the Nude

At times it was difficult for the staff to deal with the misbehavior of the emotionally disturbed prisoners. When threats or confinement to one's room did not work, there was a marble slab, with strong metal attachments at the head and the foot, where a prisoner could be chained by hand and foot. Those so chained were either stripped to their underwear or stripped totally nude and shackled to the marble slab. At times this was done with patients who were threatening to commit suicide or to hurt themselves, and the nudity was justified on the grounds that the prisoner might use clothing to hurt himself. At other times it was used for punishment of recalcitrant prisoners. Criminals can be very resistant to authority, and when you add that some were psychotic and the rest emotionally disturbed, their psychopathology could be an additional reason for defiant or out of control behavior.

A black, paranoid schizophrenic prisoner once asked me, "Why do they make us be nude in there?" and I replied, "I don't know." His answer was, "They like to see niggers naked" (about 33% of the prisoners were black, about 33% Hispanic, and about 33% white). I said, "That is not the reason," to which he replied, "Of course it is. They like to see niggers naked." The word "they" would have referred to all the staff, guards and therapists alike, as there was a window where anyone walking by could look in, as there was on all the prisoners' rooms.

Using this room for punishment seemed to involve a feeling of power on the part of the staff and a social stripping process, whereby the prisoner is stripped of his dignity and self-importance. The staff seemed to be saying: Since you won't obey, we are going to show you who is boss. You are nothing and we are in charge. Incidentally, the therapy staff never ordered anyone into this room. This was considered the province of the guards (Youth Counselors and other security staff). The Youth Counselors and the other guards primarily identified themselves as police (technically "peace officers") and some were not hesitant to employ harsh punishment with prisoners who disobeyed. Many believed in punishment for these prisoners and did not believe in treatment, even though they were working in a prison treatment program, and were supposed to provide counseling as part of their job. Sometimes, when the psychotherapists had to work in group therapy with a Youth Counselor as co-therapist, the Youth Counselor would be so ineffective or negative that treatment was difficult. At other times, however, they might be useful co-therapists.

Screaming

The prison treatment program had the reputation among prisoners at other facilities as being nicer than the regular prisons, and many prisoners wanted to be in it. Some would fake mental illness to get into our program, although this could usually be detected, and they would be sent back. One reason the treatment program was considered desirable was that there were many more staff, and the safety of the prisoner from other prisoners was more assured. In regular prisons, tough prisoners, often gang members, exploit the weaker prisoners by theft, beatings, or rape. With the exception of theft, which was rampant in our prison, the beatings and rapes could, it appeared, mostly be avoided. However, many prisoners hated our program and wanted to go back to the regular program. Their main complaint was the fact that many of the guards screamed at them to get compliance. Many of these prisoners had been screamed at by abusive parents, and this was probably a reminder of this unpleasant past. Also, screaming per se is unpleasant. The staff psychiatrist and I were in charge of treatment. We tried to get the staff to impose needed penalties against the prisoners in a dispassionate way, but many of the staff persisted in screaming. Not all staff did this, but many did, including one of the Senior Youth Counselors (in other words, the co-chief guard). Thus, this Senior Youth Counselor was a model to subordinates to use the same approach.

The prisoners already seemed to be losers in life who were unable to fit in with regular society. By screaming at them, the guards further reinforced the notion that the prisoners were like dogs—people undeserving of respect. Although the guards often felt that getting obedience in this fashion would make the prisoners into more conforming people, this would actually make them more likely to engage in antisocial acts or maintain hostility toward authority, since it was (1) yet another example of the hostility of authority toward them and (2) might further reinforce their already low self esteem, which seemed to have the effect of making them think that they were worthless and could not fit into legitimate society. Beyond all this, it seems a cruel way to treat anyone, especially those with psychosis or emotional disturbance. To make them more pro-social, I would advocate raising their self-esteem, not with regard to being a criminal, but with regard to being a person of worth who could contribute to society. This is difficult to do with this population, but a fundamental part of attempting to achieve it would be to treat the youth with some dignity.

Part of the screaming was not meant by the guards to do anything to improve the pro-social nature of the prisoners. It was just what the guards considered an effective way to achieve compliance, or a habit they had gotten into when prisoners did not comply with orders. Also, I believe it was reinforcing to the guards, since they may not have been able to scream at their wives, husbands (many of the guards were women), or whoever, but here was a group of outcasts on whom they could safely take out their frustrations.

Admitting Your Crime

The third coercive method was probably the most effective in terms of gaining compliance, and also the most justifiable. To be paroled, or to even be considered doing well in the prison treatment program, prisoners had to "admit to your commit-ment offense." Thus, one could not deny one's crime and expect to get out any time soon, or even be positively rein-forced by staff. This approach was so effective that, in my nearly two years there, I can only recall two prisoners saying that they were not guilty of the crime for which they had been convicted. And the one I worked with as therapist did not say this to the parole board, but rather confessed to it. Even this prisoner, a black member of the Crips gang, admitted to me in therapy that he was a major drug dealer, but claimed that the police planted drugs on him when they stopped his car, and thus he was not guilty of the specific offense for which he had been convicted. Thus, the belief that a prison is filled with men who claim their innocence was not true in our program. All the youth admitted to what they had been accused of, with one exception being the Crip who admitted that he was, in fact, a drug dealer; the other exception was a youth I seldom worked with who was convicted of rape but claimed he had consent. I worked in individual and group psychotherapy with many sex offenders, and although they initially used much denial and minimization about what they actually did, they all admitted to having committed their offenses.

Forcing people to admit their offense could be undesirable if the person was, in fact, innocent. However, with guilty people it seems like a good approach. How can they face up to what they have done if they continue to insist they are innocent? Thus, all the reinforcements were based on the prisoner admitting what he/she did, and this brought about compliance, which could then be used in therapy to obtain a greater understanding of the prisoner. Especially with sex offenders, we would often get initial denial about the crime ("She really wanted it" type statements), but after therapy where we demanded that they acknowledge their commitment offense, even the sex offenders would admit to what they had done, without as much defensiveness. Partly, we had the benefit of the fact that we wrote reports for the parole board, and it was known that the parole board would not parole them unless they had "dealt with their commitment offense." This does not mean that they all became cured and are now non-sex offenders (Eisenman 1991a, 1991c), but it seems like a necessary first step in dealing with any prisoners if reform is to be attempted. From working with sex offenders and criminals in general, I believe that most are unlikely to change without massive attempts at changing their antisocial orientation to life. Psychotherapy can be a first step, but there is a need for follow-up and guidance once they get back into the community. Unfortunately, this is seldom done. It is, in theory, done for those on parole; and, in some instances, it is done in practice. Typically, however, the parole agent has such a large caseload that any detailed work with the parolee is impossible.

Conclusions

In some ways, the prison treatment program functioned like the simulated prison reported on in the Zimbardo/Stanford prison study (Haney, Banks, and Zimbardo 1988) where "guards" overtly brutalized the "prisoners." From seeing a film of that experiment, shown by Zimbardo, I got the impression that the brutality was constant and based on the whims of the guards. In our program, the abuse was usually based on the prisoner first misbehaving, and may have happened less often than in the Zimbardo simulation. However, the shackling of prisoners, often in the nude, and the constant screaming at them, was physical and psychological punishment of an unnecessary nature. Correctional treatment can work (Andrews, Bonta, Cullen, Gendreau, Hoge and Zinger 1990) but it is imperative that it not be attempted in an inhumane fashion. Also, it seems that multimodal approaches, where the family can be involved and many problems of the offender are addressed, have the best chance for successfully getting the person to avoid reoffending. Henggeler and Borduin (1990) and Skonovd and Krause (1991) reported success with offenders, using approaches which involve therapists in many aspects of the offender's life, including involvement of the family. The major problem in the prison treatment program discussed here is that the non-therapy staff did not have a treatment orientation, and so used their usual, punitive approaches. Training of guards, Youth Counselors (who are really guards with a little counseling thrown into their job description), and other non-therapists could lead toward a more effective and humane treatment program. This will not, however, be an easy task, because the people who are recruited to the security staff positions typically come from a lower socioeconomic class background, and have learned a punitive, perhaps authoritarian style for managing people. When the people they have to deal with are antisocial, psychotic, and/or emotionally disturbed, they have their hands full, and resort to what seems to them to be the proper approach for handling such strange people. Also, some believed that the prisoners were bad people, incapable of changing, who thus deserved extra punishment for their misdeeds. Throw in the personal satisfaction, which dominating others can sometimes bring, and you have a situation in which abuse will occur.

Why Did the Therapists Not Do More to Prevent the Abuse?

A major question is why I and the other therapists did not do more to prevent the kinds of abuses outlined above. There are two reasons which I have been able to discern:

1. Initially, I was shocked by the marble slab and the idea of chaining someone to it as punishment. During my first week at the prison, I told a social worker, who was one of the treatment program therapists, "I am going to work to have that marble slab eliminated. It is inhumane." She said, "It is great to have new people with new ideas and new perspectives." However, a year later I told someone interviewing for a job as a therapist, "This slab looks inhumane, but what else are you going to do when dealing with violent, misbehaving prisoners?" Thus, the first explanation is that one gets used to what initially horrifies. This may be the operation of the psychological principle of adaptation. The first time we hear a loud noise, we are startled. Later, repeated loud noises, if following the first within a certain time period, have less of an effect. I believe the same thing operated here, possibly in conjunction with number two.

2. Prisons tend to operate as both bureaucratic and authoritarian institutions. Change is very difficult to achieve, and is actively prevented by many in positions of power. Also, therapists are outsiders, as the traditional prison mission is security. Even if therapy is made part of a program, security and control are given first priority. Within the framework of an authoritarian, bureaucratic setting, almost any kind of change is unlikely, especially that which is based on tender-minded things like therapy or humanism, as opposed to tough-minded things like preventing escapes or keeping order. Thus, I and all of the therapists knew, at some level, that it was unlikely we could make any change occur with regard to how guards meted out punishment. We could not even get them to take a less punitive attitude toward the prisoners, although some of us tried.

Thus, the combination of one and two is a powerful effect, co-opting the therapists into accepting what goes on. In this way, good people may stand by while evil is done. That seems less surprising to me now, given my experiences at the prison and this analysis of what could and could not be achieved. In fact, after I left the prison, I got an anonymous letter from someone who worked there, saying it was too dangerous for him to sign his name, and suggesting that my criticisms in Eisenman (1990) were valid, but had I tried to do much about them while I was at the prison, I could have been fired. Prisons tend not to tolerate questioning of the status quo, and there are all kinds of rules which can be interpreted to indicate insubordination or failure to perform duties if they are out to get you.

References

Andrews, D. A., J. Bonta, F. T. Cullen, P. Gendreau, R. D. Hoge, and I. Zinger. 1990. Does correctional treatment work? A clinically relevant and psychologically informed metaanalysis. *Criminology, 28*, 369–404.

Eisenman, R. 1990. Six problems of a prison psychologist: A personal account. *Psychological Reports, 67*, 755–761.

———. 1991a. *From crime to creativity: Psychological social factors in deviance.* Dubuque, IA: Kendall/Hunt.

———. 1991b. I worked in a prison: An insider's story. *Psychology: A Journal of Human Behavior, 28* (3/4), 22–26.

———. 1991c. Monitoring and postconfinement treatment of sex offenders: An urgent need. *Psychological Reports, 69*, 1089–1090.

———. 1992. Treatment of incarcerated offenders: Possibilities and problems. *Acta Paedopsychiatrica, 55*, 159–162.

Haney, C., C. Banks, and P. Zimbardo. 1988. A study of prisoners and guards in a simulated prison. In E. Aronson, ed. *Readings about the social animal* (5th edit., pp. 52–67). New York: W. H. Freeman.

Henggeler, S. W., and C. M. Borduin. 1990. *Family therapy and beyond: A multisystematic approach to treating the behavior problems of children and adolescents.* Belmont, CA: Wadsworth.

Skonovd, N., and W. A. Krause. 1991. The Regional Youth Educational Facility: A promising short-term intensive institutional and aftercare program for juvenile court wards. In T. L. Armstrong, ed. *Intensive interventions with high-risk youths: Promising approaches in juvenile probation and parole* (pp. 395–422). Monsey, NY: Criminal Justice Press.

Characteristics of Adolescent Felons in a Prison Treatment Program

XOX XOX XOX XOX XOX XOX XOX XOX XOX XOX XOX XOX XOX XOX

For almost two years I worked as Senior Clinical Psychologist in a California state prison treatment program for youthful male offenders. Duties included individual and group therapy and writing parole board reports. The inmates were all felony offenders and most had been previously arrested many times. From this experience I learned a great deal about their personalities, their backgrounds, and other things which should be helpful to people trying to work with or understand this population.

Since adult criminality often has its genesis in juvenile offending (Eisenman 1991a), understanding young offenders may give us insights into criminals in general, as well as the special problems of juvenile offenders. Recent studies of young offenders have provided important insights into this group (Armistead, Wierson, Forehand, and Frame 1992; Blaske, Borduin, Henggeler, and Mann 1989; Clark 1992; Eisenman 1991a, 1991b, 1992b, in press; Henggeler, Hanson, Borduin, Watson, Brunk 1985; Males 1992; Muster 1992).

Method

The prison treatment program consisted of forty-three beds for male offenders. Ages ranged from fourteen to twenty-five years old, with a modal age of sixteen years old when I did the study. There were about one-third each of blacks, Hispanics and whites. To be in the treatment program, the youth had to be judged emotionally disturbed. Thus, few of the close to 8,000 prisoners in the entire state youth prison system received treatment, as there were only three intensive treatment programs, each with about forty-three inmates. My observations were based on information, which I gained in individual and group therapy sessions, from their case files, and from information provided by other therapists. To increase the probability of having valid observations, all conclusions are (a) based on information gained by me and verified with at least one other therapist and (b) those which occurred for more than 50% of the population.

Antisocial Orientation

The youth had all developed antisocial orientations. They saw crime as the right thing to do, and people were basically objects to be manipulated or to use for one's own purposes. They might have a friend, a companion, a fellow criminal, etc. However, most of them did not have the same humane regard for others, which the more typical member of society might possess. Instead, others were to be used, and the prisoner was incredibly self-centered in trying to see that his interests were fulfilled. They often lacked the usual reciprocity which exists in friendship relationships, and would fulfill this obligation as much as they felt it was necessary to get what they wanted. In other words, if we have any kind of friendship or even professional relationship, then if I help you, you are likely to help me, and vice versa. These youth would do that to an extent, but the main basis seemed to be "What's in it for me?" Some fit this pattern more than others. For those who fit it less, they seemed able to establish friendly relationships with others without being so self-centered and exploitive.

Authority figures, in particular, were sources of problems for the inmates. While many would establish good relationships in individual therapy, they tended to have hostility toward all authority. Attitudes towards their therapists would sometimes reflect this outlook, especially in group therapy, where the group and not the therapist became the salient reference point, and the prisoner would be disobedient and hostile to impress his buddies. But in individual therapy they would often establish good relationships with their therapist and thus might be subject to influence by the therapist. Other authority figures, such as guards, teachers, the police, and authority in general were often seen as the enemy.

Not Knowing How to Be Anything Else

One of the tragedies of their lives was that most of them had no idea how to be anything other than what they were, namely full-time, hard-core criminals. Some of them may have wanted their lives to be different, but they lacked any sense of how they could change. Many of the obvious avenues available to the "straight people" were more or less closed to them. For example, education is a way of making it in our society. But many of these youth were severely deficient in academic ability. School had been a constant source of failure for them. They were often hyperactive in grammar school and learned little, and had seen school as a place where they were failures, getting bad grades and being punished by teachers. It would be useful to know if this hyperactivity is an inherent physiological disorder they suffered from, or simply boredom with normal routine. In either case, school was an imposition on many of them and something they had low self-esteem about, feeling they could not succeed in educational pursuits.

Many of them had low intelligence, with the average IQ being about 85, according to reports in their files or tests done directly on them by the psychological staff. Different tests were used to assess IQ, but as a group the inmates tended to score below the average IQ of 100. Obtaining a high school degree would be a difficult achievement for them. Although a few of them had average or above-average intelligence, they nevertheless saw school as something they were not good at. It remains an open question whether this was due strictly to hyperactivity, which made them unable to compete successfully with others, or whether an early antisocial orientation made them unwilling to sit still and listen to the teacher. Whatever the cause, their limited academic achievement and distaste for education puts them at a disadvantage in competition for decent jobs, and makes crime seem attractive as a way to make money.

At the prison, we tried to teach them how one could make it in the real world without resorting to crime. Thus, there was a therapy group called Life Planning, in which the inmates were shown how to apply for jobs, how to come to work on time, and the various skills necessary to make it in the world of work. Most of them had little idea of how to function in non-criminal society, so the criminal lifestyle was the easy and obvious option for them. Even if they were interested in a conventional, non-criminal lifestyle, the way the entire prison system was structured was that we did therapy and taught job application skills, but actual training for skills was absent from our institution. Instead, such training could be obtained at other state prisons known as training schools, which lacked the therapy programs. Thus, we could teach them how to apply for jobs and how to overcome their anger or drug abuse, but that was at the expense of actually learning job skills, which occurred in other prisons that did little or nothing about teaching them how to get along with others, avoid drugs, etc.

Family Background

One of the most revealing things about these criminals was the horrible family backgrounds they came from. Almost all of them had been subjected to physical, psychological, or sexual abuse while growing up. Typically, this had come from one or both of their parents, usually the father. The original authority in their life, their parents, had failed miserably in the socialization process. Over half had been raised by their mother only, with the father having left years ago.

Another thing that predisposed many, although not all, of them to crime was that often the parents were either criminals themselves, or at least were less than totally law-abiding. For example, many of the youth came from parents who used cocaine. In some cases the parents encouraged their children to use drugs with them, or at least saw drug usage by their kids as no big deal.

Gang Membership

Over half the black or Hispanic prisoners were members of street gangs. Blacks were members of the Crips or the Bloods, while Hispanics were members of various gangs. These gangs were like the Mafia; once you are in, there is no leaving the gang. The gangs were typically antisocial, criminal organizations, which were into committing crimes. Some like the Crips were financing themselves by controlling or attempting to control the drug trade—especially cocaine. Life was cheap to the gangs. Someone who failed to give up his wallet, or a rival gang member who tried to intrude on their territory, might be readily killed, with no remorse.

Less than 50% of the white inmates were gang members, but those who were tended to be either Skinheads or Stoners. Skinheads were racist, neo-Nazi, pro-violence groups; they were highly prejudiced and extremely anti-black and anti-Jewish. They loved fighting and proclaiming the superiority of the white race. Stoners were pro-drugs, with their name coming from the expression for getting intoxicated on drugs, "getting stoned." Most of the Stoners were mainly into drug usage and occasional burglaries to support their drug habits. They tended to be the least violent of the gangs in our prison.

Discussion

The findings suggest that the youthful offenders were tragic victims of a society into which they could not fit. Typically having low intelligence, at least as measured by the tests, being hyperactive in grammar school, and being abused by dysfunctional or criminal parents, they drifted into a life of crime and found it satisfying, in that they could be successful here and receive rewards. Alternatives to a criminal lifestyle are not apparent to them. Thus, in some ways, they are victims and deserving of our sympathy. At the same time, they have developed into people who oppose society and are willing to hurt others to get what they want. And because they have little or no remorse, they are very dangerous.

Therapy might be useful to help them reorient themselves into productive workers in our society, without being antisocial criminals. But the task at hand is very difficult, given both their lack of motivation and low level of skills. Job training, education, and help in learning how to dress for an interview, how to talk to the boss, and how to come to work on time, are all skills which most of them need, and a complete treatment program should endeavor to provide all of this, along with therapy for particular problems, e.g., drug abuse, sex offending, etc. However, in the state system in which I worked, job training was provided in the training schools, which did not provide therapy, while the treatment program provided therapy but had no means of teaching skills which would lead to employment.

Conclusions

An understanding of characteristics of adolescent felons provides some insight into what needs to be done. However, they are a difficult group to work with, and prisons are so security oriented and so not oriented toward treatment that treatment issues often get set aside, and treatment personnel may be made to feel like second-class citizens (Eisenman 1992a, 1992b). Staff burnout is frequent in prisons, both in treatment and non-treatment facilities.

A realistic look at these adolescent felons suggests the need for both (a) more sympathy for the way they have been treated and (b) more understanding of their potential for dangerousness, given their limited conscience development. Although many of the prisoners in the present study were conduct disorders and probably typical of the general prison population, the fact that they had to be deemed emotionally disturbed to get into the treatment program could mean they are different than the typical prisoner, at least in some ways.

References

Armistead, L., R. Forehand, C. Frame, M. Wierson. 1992. Psychopathology in incarcerated juvenile delinquents: Does it extend beyond externalizing problems? *Adolescence, 27*, 309–314.

Blaske, D. M., C. M. Borduin, S. W. Henggeler, and B. J. Mann. 1989. Individual, family, and peer characteristics of adolescent sex offenders and assaultive offenders. *Developmental Psychology, 25*, 846–855.

Clark, C. M. 1992. Deviant adolescent subcultures: Assessment strategies and clinical interventions. *Adolescence, 27*, 283–293.

Eisenman, R. 1991a. *From crime to creativity: Psychological and social factors in deviance.* Dubuque, IA: Kendall/Hunt.

———. 1991b. Is justice equal: A look at restitution, probation or incarceration in six states. *Louisiana Journal of Counseling and Development, 11* (2), 47–50.

——— 1992a. Administrative control of prison therapists: use of a variable-interval punishment schedule. *Psychological Reports, 71,* 146.

———. 1992b. Treatment of incarcerated offenders: Possibilities and problems. *Acta Paedopsychiatrica, 55,* 159–162.

———. In press. Living with a psychopathic personality: Case history of a successful anti-social personality. *Acta Paedopsychiatrica.*

Henggeler, S. W., C. M. Borduin, M. A. Brunk, C. L. Hanson, and S. M. Watson. 1985. Mother-son relationships of juvenile felons. *Journal of Consulting and Clinical Psychology, 53,* 942–943.

Males, M. 1992. The code blue report: Call to action or unwanted "dirism?" *Adolescence, 27,* 273–282.

Muster, N. J. 1992. Treating the victim-turned-offender. *Adolescence, 27,* 441–450.

Creativity and Impulsivity:
The Deviance Perspective

XOX XOX XOX XOX XOX XOX XOX XOX XOX XOX XOX XOX XOX XOX

When considering the relationship between creativity and impulsivity, the deviance perspective is quite useful. But first, consider the following vignettes. Ask yourself, which one of the following people is most likely to be creative?

Vignette 1: Kelly

Kelly is a professor who is very precise. When Kelly teaches, things are spelled out quite definitely: this is the concept, there are three aspects, also here is a related concept, with two aspects, etc. Kelly can be described as methodical. In both personal and professional life, Kelly likes to have things clear and definite. If there is not clarity, Kelly seeks to find it.

Vignette 2: Chris

Chris is also a professor, but is not always precise. Although Chris has stimulating ideas and colleagues and students are sometimes impressed if not awed by his mind, at times Chris seems to dart from one thing to another. Chris may be working on one idea and then suddenly something sparks him off in another direction, onto a totally different idea. He drops the first task and takes up the second.

**Stop here and do not proceed until you have
decided who is more likely to be creative.**

Have you answered this question? Well, if so, I can tell you that it is something of a trick question. I tried to make Vignette 1: Kelly be someone who is not impulsive and Vignette 2: Chris to be someone who is impulsive. But—and here is the trick part—from my work in creativity I would say that both have an equal chance to be creative or not creative. I suspect that people who know nothing about the creativity literature might be tempted to pick Vignette 1: Kelly as the more likely creative, due to the orderliness of her mind. However, people who study creativity know that orderliness can be counter-productive when trying to come up with original solutions, and might prefer Vignette 2: Chris, who displays the intensity and nonconformity, which sometimes characterize creative people. However, I wish to maintain most strongly that there are many pathways to creativity. Novel, original solutions may come from one who is very precise and orderly or from one who is very impulsive but with a good mind. Also, either orderliness or impulsivity may be harmful to the development of creativity. I hope you will forgive my trick question if it makes the point that creativity can be facilitated or impaired by orderliness, and the same is true for impulsivity.

Perhaps more needs to be said about how impulsiveness can facilitate creativity. I feel that impulsivity has gotten a bad reputation, being associated with crime, poor thinking skills, and the like. Consider this quote from a book by Hollin (1990) on young offenders, explaining the Ross and Fabiano (1985) description of cognitive styles of offenders: "*Impulsivity* is defined by Ross and Fabiano as the omission of thought between impulse and action. This lack of reflection may be due to a variety of causes: a failure to learn to stop and think, a failure to learn 'effective thinking,' or a failure to generate alternative responses" (Hollin 1990). If this is the definition of impulsivity, then impulsivity would be associated with a lack of creativity (generation of alternatives is often one of the measures of creativity) and a general inability to function well in society. However, if we take a less extreme view of impul-sivity and view it as quick action with limited reflection, then, under certain circumstances impulsivity might be useful. Dickman (1990) is thinking along similar lines, and has distin-guished between functional and dysfunctional impulsivity. Under the old view of impulsivity as a negative trait, Finch, Saylor and Spirito (1982) found impulsivity associated with behavior problems. But using the Dickman (1990) distinction, Schaeffer and Lester (1992) found that there was no difference between normal and problem students in dysfunctional impulsivity, but that students with behavioral problems showed less functional impulsivity than the normal students. This is not at all an obvious finding, and shows the utility of distinguishing between functional and dysfunctional impulsivity. Thus, impulsivity, at least certain kinds on certain occasions, can be helpful.

I will return to a discussion of impulsivity, especially as it relates to creativity, but it will be helpful to look at a concept psychologists almost never consider: deviance. Since impulsiveness is typically viewed negatively, the impulsive person may often be seen as deviant and condemned. An examination of the deviance concept will allow a greater understanding of how impulsivity is often viewed negatively, and how this leads to an irrational condemnation of impulsive people. At times, impulsivity is undesirable, but it also has functional, desirable qualities.

Deviance

Deviance is a concept that sociologists have looked at—although often in a flawed manner; it is also a concept that psychologists almost never use—at least not in the way I discuss it here. Thus, the addition of the deviance perspective, without the flaws of the typical sociological approach, can add perspective. Psychologists have typically studied certain manifestations of deviance, e.g., mental illness. But this is not the same as looking at, say, mental illness from a deviance perspective. From the psychologist's perspective, a person is mentally disordered if he/she meets certain criteria set forth in the American Psychiatric Association's (1987) manual of diagnostic terms, or if they fit certain images we have of the mentally ill. The deviance perspective would add to this by looking at how the person is labeled as mentally ill, and whether there might be variables which make some people considered mentally disordered, while others with the same behaviors and problems are not seen as mentally disordered. For example, perhaps lower class individuals are likely to be labeled mentally ill, while middle and upper class people escape this labeling some of the time, despite identical problems. Or, perhaps in some instances women would be seen as more/less disturbed than men when the problem is the same.

Sociologists who study deviance have been very good about seeing these nuances while psychologists have been, in my opinion, less likely to look at the social factors that result in the official classification of people. However, there has been a terrible flaw in the sociological approach (Eisenman 1991a). With a few exceptions, sociologists have seen deviance as something bad, while deviance should simply mean different. Thus, creativity is deviance because it involves statistically infrequent behavior. The person who is independent in a conforming group is deviant, but perhaps in a good way. The person in the lynch mob who says, "This is wrong. We should not do this," is deviant. Deviants often face pressure to conform and if they do not they are subject to all kinds of pressures, which ultimately could involve such things as being fired, being dropped from the group, having legal sanctions brought against them, or, in the extreme case, being killed.

There have been different theories of deviance, with perhaps the most interesting being labeling theory. Labeling theory goes too far, in my opinion, in claiming that the main reason a person is seen as being locked into the deviant role is the labeling process (Little 1989). I believe that extroverts are often different than introverts, that liberals are often different than conservatives, and so forth. Sociologists may have a hard time seeing this or dealing with it because their field typically defines things in social terms, and personality explanations would thus be unacceptable. To say, for example, that the only reason some people are sent to prison is that they have been labeled as criminals overlooks their criminal behavior. On the other hand, it is useful to see how the labeling process occurs. If we do this, then we find that the labeling is often unfair. For example, I looked at data on punishment of 876 offenders from six jurisdictions (Eisenman 1991b). The sentences involved incarceration, probation, or restitution. The punishments varied greatly, suggesting that, in part, the sentencing of these serious, repeat offenders was based on where the court was located. In Ada County (Boise) Idaho, no offender received probation; while in Oklahoma County (Oklahoma City) Oklahoma and Dane County (Madison) Wisconsin, none of the offenders was incarcerated. While some of the findings might be due to non-comparable samples, the major thrust of the data is to suggest that what sentence a juvenile offender gets depends on where he receives his trial, which is hardly a fair result. The sentence should reflect the needs of the offender, and of the community, including the victim. But the findings show that some places have a tough law-and-order, lock 'em up approach, while others are lenient, with perhaps a view of "these are just kids." Thus, a look at how people are processed is crucial, and much is left out if we conclude, consciously or unconsciously, that crime can be understood by saying that criminals are people who commit crimes, without considering how society labels and deals with them. Do you doubt that the police and/or the criminal justice system may treat differently the middle or upper class kid caught breaking into a building vs. the lower class kid doing the same thing? Labeling theory would say that the lower class kid is more likely to become a career criminal as a result of being defined as a criminal by the system and treated as such.

At times, the public and professional perception of deviance can be quite arbitrary. Consider the concept of "sexual acting out." This concept is used widely in psychiatry, psychology, and other fields, but is actually somewhat vague. Freud (1914/1946) wrote of acting out meaning that the patient expresses in action what is forgotten or repressed. He seems to mean that instead of talking things out with the psychoanalyst, the patient may do something, outside the therapy situation, which is not socially acceptable. Others have used the concept in a similar fashion or modified it to suit their purposes (Altman 1957; Fenichel 1945; Greenacre 1950; Kanzer 1957; Rosenfeld 1966). Since sex is a highly emotional topic, the term "sexual acting out" has all of the ambiguities of "acting out" along with the emotive aspects. I found that in both a state mental hospital and at a university clinic, "sexual acting out" was typically used to describe women but not men (Eisenman 1987). This would seem to represent professionals contributing to the sexual double standard, whereby certain behaviors are seen as acceptable for men but not for women. The professionals do not realize they are doing this, but they bring with them the cultural baggage which discriminates against females, and so use the term "sexual acting out" in a biased manner. There was also a statistically non-significant tendency for the term to be used more with regard to homosexual males than with regard to heterosexual males. Again, the professional is probably unaware of holding prejudiced beliefs, but when using a somewhat vague term such as "sexual acting out," the learned prejudices come through. Thus, female sexuality, or male homosexuality, may be seen as deviant in the eyes of the greater society—at least when people are thinking in prejudiced, stereotyped fashion about these topics. The professions, unwittingly I suspect, support the social prejudices by the biased way in which they describe female sexuality and male homosexuality as sexual acting out. Thus, the term "sexual acting out" functions as a moral judgment as well as a diagnostic (in the broad sense of "diagnosis") term.

In some instances, the person accused of sexual acting out is probably no different than the person not so accused. The person simply has the misfortune of having the label attached to him/her. But on other occasions, there may be a real difference between the labeled person and the non-labeled person. The person accused of sexual acting out may be more impulsive in regard to his/her sexual behavior in order to take advantage of certain opportunities for sex. The person not labeled may have had similar temptations, but due to inhibitions does not partake. Thus, there may be, at times, a real behavioral difference between the person labeled as deviant and the person not so labeled. But, there may be no real moral difference between the two. The person who takes advantage of a taboo or quasi-taboo sexual opportunity is not necessarily any more immoral than a more inhibited counterpart. This is so because many of society's rules about sexual behavior are overly rigid.

Our society has amazingly contradictory teachings about sex. On the one hand, it is pervasive in the entertainment fields, such as movies and television, and in the sexy way many people dress. The message seems to be: do it. On the other hand, we have, at the same time, inhibitory messages, many of them due to our Puritanical heritage, which says: don't do it. Such contradictions are hardly conducive to good mental health or a stress-free life. Many normal people have sexual problems, while there are also people for whom their sexual behavior reflects a disorder (American Psychiatric Association 1987). For people with inhibited sexual behavior, external influences or use of fantasy can increase sexual behavior. This use of fantasy can even increase sexual behavior in normal individuals (Eisenman 1982). However, sexually disturbed people can also use fantasy to increase antisocial sexual behavior, such as child molestation or rape. Our society's contradictory messages about sex can lead to horrible consequences, as when fraternity boys gang rape an intoxicated female guest.

The fraternity gang rape instances are based on (a) misperceptions, which you probably already knew, as when the fraternity members think the woman has indicated willingness but she believes she has not and (b) on intentional gang rape plans. Of the two explanations, (b) is more interesting because it says that seemingly normal boys are behaving not only in horrible fashion, but with intent. Yet, Sanday (1991), in her anthropological study of a fraternity, found that the members planned "pulling train" (gang rape) and did not simply fall into it due to miscommunication. Unless it could be shown that some or all of the fraternity boys had antisocial personalities, the explanation would have to be in terms of the social norms and how *good* people can learn to do *evil* things if their society encourages them. Were this not so, it would be impossible to get a large number of soldiers to fight and kill the enemy in war time.

Another example of social norms leading to inappropriate sexual or aggressive behavior involves college athletes. It appears that college athletes are often accused of acquaintance rape or other anti-social behaviors. Such charges are difficult to prove, as it is often the victim's word against the assailant, with no witnesses, and the athletes are usually either (a) not prosecuted or (b) acquitted. I think of the University of Minnesota basketball players who were twice prosecuted for rape and acquitted both times; a University of Cincinnati basketball player who was tried and acquitted for date rape, and who had previously been accused or date rape by a woman who chose not to prosecute; and a recent case involving two LSU football players, who severely beat a Louisiana State University student, and also hit his female companion. Even though they broke his jaw, damaged his car, and apparently beat him quite severely (one report said there were bruises covering all of his body), the football players were given one year probation by the judge, with the conviction to be deleted from their records if the one year is successfully completed (Associated Press 1992; Talley 1992). The judge was apparently impressed with the argument of one of the defense attorneys that his client was making much better grades now, was remorseful, and in counseling, including substance abuse counseling. Such lenient sentences, or the more typical non-prosecution, sends a message that athletes have status and can get away with crimes. Also, athletics typically involves aggression and dominance as part of the game, so the athletes are socialized into learning what could be, in normal social circumstances, impulsive, antisocial behavior. There should be programs on all college campuses involving work with fraternities and athletes in an attempt to prevent rape, assault, and other antisocial behaviors, because it appears these type groups are at higher than normal risk for engaging in such behaviors.

There are other more acceptable instances of sexual behavior occurring where someone is likely to be labeled deviant due to society's harsh rules about sex. At one time it was more obviously the case than it is today that one was not supposed to engage in premarital or extramarital sex. Times have changed, perhaps not as radically as some think, but more than those who deny change would admit. People often have sex before marriage, although they may be made to feel guilty due to their religious upbringing or general social norms. In fact, one interesting phenomenon is pluralistic ignorance, where a whole peer group may be engaging in premarital intercourse, but none of them know that the others are. If there are conservative, traditional norms in their society, then all of them may feel, "I am different" or "I know it is wrong but I can't help myself." None may admit to the others what they are doing, thus keeping alive the myth that premarital sex is taboo and does not occur, at least not among nice people.

Regarding extramarital sex, the fact that someone is married is not as great a taboo against intercourse outside marriage as it once was. Thus, the world is more complex, for when the taboo was obvious, the choice was limited or absent. You just do not do that. But if marriage is not always a barrier to sex outside the marital relationship, then opportunities exist, but in a dangerous sense, since one never knows for sure whether the married partner is available or not available. Also, there could be consequences from the other partner, ranging from harsh words to homicide.

Society both encourages and condemns a wide range of sexual behavior. The person who partakes of condemned sexual behavior may be an antisocial person who is not deterred by taboos, or he/she may simply be more impulsive, creative, or liberal than the average person. Such people are often persecuted, sometimes on a selective basis, by society. By selective I mean that some of them will not be persecuted, but if others are out to get them, then their liberal sexual behavior may be used as an excuse. Or some members of society may actually be offended by the behavior, but the persecuted person is simply the unlucky one, since many others will not be persecuted. I think of a female high school teacher in Cambridge, Massachusetts who was convicted of statutory rape for having sex with a fifteen-year old male student. I watched the court trial on *Court TV*, a cable channel which shows live court cases. Someone was obviously out to get her; yet, when the case came to court she had to defend herself in terms of claiming not to have had sex with him. If a law is on the books, it does little good to say in court that it is a stupid law. Had the boy been sixteen years old there would have been no case, as sixteen is the age of consent for boys in Massachusetts. The boy was already sexually active, yet the teacher was convicted and sentenced to the state prison for women. There have also been men sent to prison for statutory rape even though the girl lied about her age and looked older than the age of consent, which varies from state to state. Thus, people who are sexually liberal, creative, impulsive, or whatever are subject to persecution by those who do not like them or who hold more conservative, inhibitory beliefs. Even doing scholarly research on sex can cause one to be labeled as deviant and subjected to unpleasant treatment from others (Fisher 1992).

The same kind of problem exists with regard to our drug laws. Our society is having a "war on drugs," which has actually been going on for some time. Since the 1960s I have been aware that some of our most creative citizens are being jailed because they experiment with or use drugs. Since creative people are more likely to experiment than would noncreative people, creative people will often try illicit drugs (Eisenman 1991a). Our drug problem is complex, and I have no desire to see more babies born addicted to cocaine, alcohol, or any other drug. The social cost is going to be tremendous. Two of the prisoners I worked with had been born addicted to cocaine, and both showed a negative kind of impulsivity which may have been due to brain deficiencies caused by their being born addicted. But making sweeping laws to indicate our displeasure with certain behaviors is not the best way to go. In fact, our drug prohibitions have made possible a large profit for organized criminals, who sell to the public what the greater society denies. There are no simple solutions, but a mindless police mentality (lock up the drug users) is not the answer and statistics about declining use of drugs may be inaccurate, given the heightened incidence of people admitted to emergency wards for drug overdoses (Avis 1990). What seems to be happening is that our government thinks the problem can be solved by creating deviance in a large percentage of the population and using them as scapegoats to say to others, "These people are terrible. Just say no to drugs." Yet, the desire to change one's consciousness is perhaps as old as history and drug usage may be a normal kind of human behavior. If so, the problem is how to regulate it so that people are not hurt. I do not want the driver of the airplane or commuter train I ride on to be high on drugs. How do we prevent this without criminalizing a large percentage of the population? Perhaps if drugs were viewed as a public health issue rather than a legal issue more creative and effective solutions could be found. We tried prohibition with regard to alcohol many years ago and it did not work, but we do not seem to learn from experience. The desire to create deviance in others and then punish them seems to be a part of our culture.

Creativity and Impulsivity

The rest of this chapter will deal with creativity per se, impulsivity per se, or the two in combination. People usually do not think of linking creativity and impulsivity, even though Fitzgerald (1966) several years ago found that creative students consider themselves impulsive. At times, I shall employ the deviance perspective (Eisenman 1991a) to throw light on the matter at hand. Remember, deviance means difference, and includes how society perceives people as different or not different.

When people write about creativity, they often write as though creativity was the same for all fields of study. I do not believe this. I think that there may be very different ways in which, for example, scientists become creative as opposed to artists. There is no doubt some similarity, but there are also differences. Creativity can be defined as originality plus usefulness. Originality is at the heart of the definition, while usefulness is needed so that an original but totally non-useful solution is not deemed creative. For example, a psychotic might say $2 + 2 = 999,890.15$. Original but not useful, thus not creative. As Piirto (1992) has pointed out, when J. P. Guilford (1950) became President of the American Psychological Association and gave a speech, which was likely the turning point in fostering interest in creativity, he qualified what he was saying about creativity by saying that his factors probably related only to creative scientists or technologists. Most people probably do not recall this qualification, or never heard of it. But it is an important distinction. Research by Feist (1991) shows the importance of considering both similarities and differences among art and science students with regard to creativity.

Forget different fields of study for the moment and consider different people. I strongly believe that there are different pathways for different people to achieve creativity. In a previous study (Eisenman 1969), summarized in my chapter on "Creativity" in my deviance book (Eisenman 1991a), I found that people scored differently on a 30-item, true-false, paper- and-pencil test of creativity I devised, which I called the Personal Opinion Survey. Some high scorers on this creativity test were high scorers because of a general openness to experience, while others were high in what I called "adventuresomeness," which some might label sensation seeking. (People who use drugs also tend to score high on adventuresomeness. See Eisenman, Grossman, and Goldstein, 1980, for a study showing greater creativity and adventuresomeness and less authoritarianism in marijuana users.) It is even more complex than that. Some high (creative) scorers tended to answer in the creative direction on items of an impersonal nature, such as philosophical beliefs, but not so much on items relating to interpersonal things, such as love. And vice versa. Thus, there may be some people who become creative due to competence in impersonal matters, but who are not interpersonally skilled or creative; while others may be interpersonally creative but less so when dealing with impersonal, abstract issues. These findings come from a cluster analysis of high-scoring (creative) subjects. I have attempted to avoid technical issues as much as possible here. The interested person is referred to my book (Eisenman 1991a) or the original article (Eisenman 1969), which goes into detail about the cluster analysis.

I hope the above has shown that there is no one correct pathway to creativity. For some it will be dogged study in the lab, for others it might involve an impulsive flight into a new idea which catches their fancy. Of course, to impulsively "fly" into an area and come up with a creative solution, one must have some skills. I do not care for the romanticized view that just anyone can be creative. To some extent that is true, but for the most part I suspect it requires a minimal amount of intelligence and learning. Thus, the creative person is likely to be a craftsman who goes against the grain, not a novice who wildly experiments. The novice, in my view, is handicapped by not having the experience or knowledge necessary to go off into wild, impulsive speculations and come up with something meaningful. Perhaps that is one reason why I found prisoners tend to be quite low in creativity (Eisenman 1992). They are certainly uninhibited in many ways, relative to the rest of us. But their educational achievement and thinking ability is usually pathetic. In my experience, from working as a prison psychologist for nearly two years, they typically come from a family background of physical, psychological, or sexual abuse, and/or from a background of criminal or less-than-honest parents. This background is hardly conducive to the playfulness and spontaneity which seems to facilitate creativity. Instead, it leads to anger, rigidity, and striking out at others.

Speaking of striking, a striking example of how impulsiveness can foster creativity was provided in a talk which Philip Zimbardo (1992) recently gave to my Addictive Behaviors class. Zimbardo, reported on unpublished research of his in which students were allowed to be impulsive in their art work. They were told to draw any way they wanted and that it was not subject to assessment, versus students who were told their art products would be assessed. Actually, experts analyzed the works of students in both groups, and while those warned that their work would be evaluated performed better in some technical categories, the art experts rated the works of the students in the no-assessment condition as more creative. Thus, Zimbardo found that impulsivity led to creativity.

I am sure that one could take the above finding and make it come out, in a different situation, where impulsivity would not result in higher creativity. For example, if a highly structured solution is required, say an accountant doing someone's income taxes, then impulsivity might lead simply to poor performance. We do not always want a nurse to be creative and go against the doctor's orders, although it is alarming that as time in nursing school increases, students become less creative (Eisenman 1970).

For those who read Polish, there is an important article by Matczak (1982) which deals with how various cognitive styles may be of use in facilitating creativity, but at different points in the creative process. She looked at individual differences in creativity as related to the cognitive styles of field independence, tolerance of cognitive instability, and reflection vs. impulsivity. Her point is that we cannot pick one cognitive style and say: this is it, as far as creativity is concerned. To elaborate on her point, I suspect that when people hear of reflection vs. impulsivity, reflection is seen as the good attribute and impulsivity as the bad one. Reflection sounds like a reasoned view of something before acting, while impulsivity sounds like jumping in without sufficient thought. Sometimes this is exactly what is happening. But there are also people inhibited by too much reflection, and there are people who feel they have to do something, and approach it in a highly motivated and perhaps impulsive fashion. But if they have the skills, the impulsivity serves as a motivating force. They feel, "I have to do this," and they go into it full force. They may disregard others or other items of business, but the impulsivity serves to make them concentrate fully on the task they have undertaken. These people seem captured by their work. They may say "The book wrote itself," or "The painting painted itself," so caught up in it all are they. Creative people often talk this way. Of course, the stereotyped impulsivity, the bad one, would be that as quickly as they undertake a task, they lose interest. If this is how the impulsivity works, then it is destructive. Such persons are not focused and may have fears about their ability to achieve anything. But, if the impulsivity serves as the motivator and they stay with the task, then the impulsivity can be very useful.

The attempt to link creativity with mental illness used to bug me. I did not believe that the mentally ill were creative. Having worked in a state mental hospital and in private practice, it seemed obvious that mental disorders interfered with productive thinking, as well as creativity. In fact, I did a study (Eisenman 1990) which showed that either physical or mental illness interfered with creativity. However, there is one kind of mental illness, manic-depression (more technically, bipolar disorder) in which there may be a creativity/mental illness link. The link seems to be due not to full-blown manic-depression, but rather to a limited mania, especially the state of hypomania, wherein the person may possess an energy and an impulsivity which is conducive to creativity (Eisenman 1991c; Richards and Kinney 1990; Schuldberg 1990). Part of the limited mania may involve negative thoughts, too, so it is a mixed blessing. My advice is, if you can help it, do not be mentally ill. But the limited mania does have facilitative aspects as well as possibly producing a harmful anxiety and paranoia. It is these facilitative aspects—the energy, the impulsive questing after thoughts which can then be turned into something—which links hypomania and creativity. As a person becomes more manic, he/she may lose the ability to concentrate or do anything useful with the rapid flow of ideas, and the disorder is then mostly or totally harmful to the person.

Speaking of not being able to use your ideas, I have an idea about students today, based on my experiences with freshmen and sophomores in my Introduction to Psychology classes. We are, at present, an open admissions university, so what I am about to say may be less true at more selective schools. Or it may still apply, given the similar mass culture exposures which people have. I find that students are often unreceptive to new ideas and seem easily bored. This is especially true when I show a film, which you might think would be entertaining to them. The films I show are educational in nature, and many students seem not to like any of them. I think that as a result of watching *MTV* (Music Television) and seeing movies such as the Arnold Schwarzenegger films or similar action movies, the students have come to expect constant action and entertainment. Thus, mere thought, no matter how interesting it might be to the teacher, fails in comparison.

Of course, the comparison of entertainment vs. education is ridiculous—the two should not be compared. Thought can seldom compete in entertainment value with mass culture entertainment except for those who have learned to use their minds and have, what is for them, interesting and exciting thoughts. For students who have not reached the point where they have exciting concepts in their minds, school is bound to be boring, except for the times when I can grab their interest by talking on something they really like, such as the hidden meaning of their dreams, or by using humor and dramatic voice qualities to hold their interest. Perhaps as they advance in college, they will get turned on to certain ideas or fields. But, at present, many of them seem impulsive in a negative sense, or at least incredibly unreflective. This is impulsiveness in a special sense, in that they do not threaten or attack me the way an impulsive prisoner might. Rather, their minds are impulsive, in that anything that does not reach a high degree of entertainment value is likely to be disregarded. Perhaps I am being somewhat unfair. After all, some do make As or Bs, which suggest that they are learning something. The above argument would hold better if no one ever made better than a C. However, I suspect I am on to something.

Others have said that today's youth seem uninterested in, for example, working in a laboratory setting to learn how to do research. The psychologist who made this statement contrasted them with students of yesterday—whenever that was—who were more willing to put up with the unexciting aspects of research in order to learn about it. And, he is at an elite university, so perhaps it is unrelated to SAT or ACT scores. If he and I are correct, perhaps our culture is inducing a kind of negative impulsiveness, making people want immediate, fun stimulation. Since few things in life provide that, these people are bound to be disappointed much of the time. If they are not willing to serve their apprenticeship, so to speak, and learn the details or research, or a new language, or a new book, or whatever, then they will never get to the point where any of it seems interesting or worth doing. I can imagine them in therapy saying, "Nothing interests me." If this is a general cultural phenomenon, then I would expect creativity to be in decline, since I think creativity typically is built on a foundation of acquired skills.

I previously mentioned that prisoners tend to be low in creativity (Eisenman 1992). There are occasional exceptions; unfortunately, the exceptions tend to be in the area of crime. Some prisoners have creative skills when it comes to being a criminal. People who use their creative and impulsive tendencies for horrible purposes are said to have antisocial personality disorder. This is the proper term (American Psychiatric Association 1987) for what used to be called psychopaths, and then later, sociopaths. The antisocial personality is impulsive, without conscience, has little or no anxiety, and no empathy for others, although he/she may be clever in sizing up others in order to manipulate them. Here is clearly a case where impulsivity serves evil purposes. I will, present one brief case history, which took place in the city where I live and teach, Lake Charles, Louisiana (a mostly peaceful, low-crime-rate city), and involved as victim a student from my university, McNeese State University.

A young man, subsequently diagnosed at his murder trial as an antisocial personality disorder, got out of prison after serving a brief term for the rape of his sister. He went to a very popular local nightclub where young people go to dance. He met the McNeese State student and either persuaded her to go with him or abducted her. We do not know. He took her to a field where he raped her, cut out her eyes so she could not identify him, and then choked her to death. At his trial, his public defender pleaded that his life be spared because he had a diagnosed mental disorder, and the public defender said the disorder could be treated.

Of course, what is misleading here is that while antisocial personality is listed in the American Psychiatric Association's (1987) manual of mental disorders, it is not a mental illness in the way we think of such things, but refers to someone who is legally sane and has the qualities which I previously mentioned. Thus, it is misleading to plead for mercy by calling antisocial personality a mental disorder. Also, most people who have worked with them, including myself, consider them basically untreatable. It used to be thought that they could not learn or at least would not learn except for monetary rewards, as opposed to social reinforcement from others. However Bernard and Eisenman (1967) showed that both assumptions are false. Their antisocial personality prisoners demonstrated learning, and learned better for the social reinforcer of the experimenter saying "good" than they did for money. However, they do not seem to change as a result of therapy. The young man was sentenced to death by lethal injection. People like him are a good argument for the death penalty, because even if they are given life in prison they can escape, demonstrate a good record in the prison and get paroled, or assault or kill guards or fellow inmates. Once paroled, they will often rape and kill again, causing great misery to others. Since they are extremely clever, even professionals are, at times, taken in by them. The antisocial personality is clearly an instance in which impulsivity has all the bad connotations.

A Final Word

Impulsivity can have harmful effects, and this is the view most of us have learned. However, as this chapter shows, impulsivity can have beneficial effects as well, including fostering creativity. Recent work has shown that infants have different temperament traits and that different parts of the brain may be involved (Kagan and Snidman 1991a, 1991b). This implies that there can be hereditary causes of impulsivity, reflection, inhibition, and the like, as well as psychological causes. We are at a fairly early stage in our understanding of impulsivity, creativity, and deviance; and they are all important topics for further research.

References

Altman, L. 1957. On the oral nature of acting out. *Journal of the American Psychoanalytic Association, 5*, 648–662.

Associated Press. 1992, May 24. Judge pleased with Jacquet's rehab. *Lake Charles American Press*, p. 22.

Avis, H. 1990. *Drugs and life*. Dubuque, IA: William C. Brown.

Bernard, J. L., and R. Eisenman. 1967. Verbal conditioning in sociopaths with social and monetary reinforcement. *Journal of Personality and Social Psychology, 6*, 203–206.

Dickman, S. J. 1990. Functional and dysfunctional impulsivity. *Journal of Personality and Social Psychology, 58*, 95–102.

Eisenman, R. 1969. Components of creativity, verbal conditioning, and risk taking. *Perceptual and Motor Skills, 39*, 687–700.

———. 1982. Sexual behavior as related to sex fantasies and experimental manipulation of authoritarianism and creativity. *Journal of Personality and Social Psychology, 43*, 853–860.

———. 1987. Sexual acting out: Diagnostic category or moral judgment? *Bulletin of the Psychonomic Society, 25*, 387–388.

———. 1987. *Diagnostic and statistical manual of mental disorders*. American Psychiatric Association.(3rd edit., rev.). Washington, DC:

———. 1990. Creativity, complexity-simplicity, and physical and mental illness. *Creativity Research Journal, 3*, 233–238.

———.1991a. *From crime to creativity: Psychological and social factors in deviance*. Dubuque, IA: Kendall/Hunt.

———. 1991b. Is justice equal?: A look at restitution, probation, or incarceration in six states. *Louisiana Journal of Counseling and Development, 11* (2), 47–50.

———. 1991c. Manic-depression and creativity. Review of D. J. Hershman and J. Lieb. The key to genius: Manic-depression and the creative life. *Creativity Research Journal, 4* 399–400.

———. 1992. Creativity in prisoners: Conduct disorder vs. psychotics. *Creativity Research Journal, 5,* 175–181.

Feist, G. J. 1991. Synthetic and analytic thought: Similarities and differences among art and science students. *Creativity Research Journal, 4,* 145–155.

Fenichel, O. 1945. Neurotic acting out. *Psychoanalytic Review, 32,* 197–206.

Finch, A. J., C. F. Saylor, and A. Spirito. 1982. Impulsive cognitive style and impulsive behavior in emotionally disturbed children. *Journal of Genetic Psychology, 141,* 293–294.

Fisher, T. D. 1992. *Confessions of a closet sex researcher.* Mount Vernon, IA: The Society for the Scientific Study of Sex. (pamphlet)

Fitzgerald, E. T. 1966. Measurement of openness to experience: A study of regression in the service of the ego. *Journal of Personality and Social Psychology, 4,* 655–663.

Freud, S. 1946. Recollection, repetition, and working through. In *Collected papers.* London Hogarth Press (original work published 1914).

Greenacre, P. 1950. General problems of acting out. *Psychoanalytic Quarterly, 19,* 445–467

Guilford, J. P. 1950. Creativity. *American Psychologist, 5,* 444–454.

Hollin, C. R. 1990. *Cognitive-behavioral interventions with young offenders.* Elmsford, MY Pergamon Press.

Kagan, J. and N. Snidman. 1991a. Infant predictors of inhibited and uninhibited profiles. *Psychological Science, 2,* 40–44.

———. (1991b). Temperamental factors in human development. *American Psychologist, 46,* 956–862,

Kanzer, M. 1957. Acting out and its relation to the impulse disorders. *Journal of the American Psychoanalytic Association, 5,* 136–145.

Little, C. G. 1989. *Deviance and control: Theory, research, and social policy.* Itasca, IL: F. E. Peacock.

Matczak, A. 1982. Indywidualne wlasciwosci funkcjonowania poznawczego jako wyznaczniki tworczosci/ Individual properties of cognitive functioning as indicators of creativity. *Psychologia-Wychowawcza, 25,* 1–14.

Piirto, J. (1992). *Understanding those who create.* Dayton, OH: Ohio Psychology Press.

Richards, R. and D. K. Kinney. 1990. Mood swings and creativity. *Creativity Research Journal, 3,* 202–217.

Rosenfeld, H. A. 1966. The need of patients to act out during analysis. *Psychoanalytic Forum, 1,* 20–25.

Ross, R. R. and E. A. Fabiano. 1985. *Time to think: A cognitive model of delinquency prevention and offender rehabilitation.* Johnson City, TN: Institute of Social Sciences and Arts.

Sanday, P. R. 1991. *Fraternity gang rape: Sex, brotherhood, and privilege on campus.* New York: New York University Press.

Schaeffler, J. and D. Lester. 1992. Impulsivity in problem students. *Psychological Reports, 70,* 10.

Schuldberg, D. 1990. Schizotypal and hypomanic traits, creativity, and psychological health. *Creativity Research Journal, 3,* 218–230.

Talley, T. 1992, May 23. LSU football player gets year of probation for role in brawl. *State-Times/Morning Advocate,* section B, p. 1.

Zimbardo, P. G. 1992. *Time perspective.* Lecture given to Dr. Russell Eisenman's Addictive Behaviors class, Spring 1992 semester McNeese State University.

Clinical Approaches to Creativity: Mental Illness and Deviance

XOX XOX XOX XOX XOX XOX XOX XOX XOX XOX XOX XOX XOX XOX

Introduction

There is a long history of beliefs that creativity and mental illness are related (Bower 1989; Grinder 1985; Wallace 1985; Zigler and Farber 1985). This belief has not been based on empirical, scientific findings but, instead, on folk wisdom about the alleged link between madness and genius. In essence, this has been a folk wisdom case history approach, since people have been aware of creative people who have shown some apparent signs of mental illness, e.g., van Gogh cutting off his ear and giving it to a prostitute. If I mention to people that I am writing about creativity and mental illness they often say something like, "Oh, yes, madness and creativity are linked." This seems to be a popular stereotype.

Several years ago, I found (Eisenman 1969b) that students believed that mental illness and creativity are related, even though they had been informed by me that such was not the case (which is what I believed at that time). Their willingness to put an answer on their test that contradicted the teacher shows how strong this belief is, since students are usually quite willing to throw back to the teacher what the teacher has said, in order to get a good grade. At the time, I thought that the alleged link of creativity and mental illness was nonsense. I had worked with the mentally ill, and they seemed the farthermost thing from creative. They seemed lost in their own tragic worlds, with distorted perceptions of reality, not in a creative fashion. Rothenberg (1990) also believes that mental illness does not facilitate creativity, but interferes with it.

Perhaps There Is a
Creativity/Mental Illness Relationship

In recent years, I have become convinced that, in some instances, there can be a relationship between creativity and mental illness, although I would not expect there to always be such a link. Perhaps it exists in certain limited instances, such as among highly talented people who also have, hypomania, an early and less severe stage in manic-depression. In the hypomanic state, the person would have a rush of energy which might allow him/her to think of many things, including some unusual things which do not seem to fit. However, the energy would allow the person to work on putting ideas together, and possibly coming come up with creative ideas and creative work.

If the hypomania advanced to full-blown mania, I would be more skeptical that the person could be productive, although he/she would have many unusual thoughts. It may be, however, that some full-blown manic-depressives (technically, bipolar disorder) can be creative even in the throes of their mania. Depression would definitely seem to diminish creativity. Have you ever seen depressed people or been very depressed yourself? Depression does not seem conducive to doing much of anything except sitting around and feeling sorry for yourself. However, Hershman and Lieb (1988) believe that depression can also foster creativity. They believe that most creativity springs from manic-depression, which is a rather radical idea. Further, they believe that the manic state can be conducive to creative production, and that the depressive state may allow for a critical sorting out of what works and what does not. Thus, in their view, the depressive part of the manic-depression can aid in creativity by putting a critical eye on the ideas produced during the manic stage. Of course, this is speculation on their part. They do not defend their position with scientific research studies, but instead point to case histories, which they say support their viewpoint. I like case histories and feel they have a place (Eisenman 1992b; Wallace 1989). I think it is terrible that it is almost impossible to get a case history published in the American Psychological Association journals, which want only scientific studies or theory based on such studies. But, alas, I must also admit that case histories can be used to prove anything you wish, hence their bad reputation in our scientifically-oriented age. And, this is what I fear Hershman and Lieb (1988) may have done in saying that case histories show that both mania and depression foster creativity. They may have selected case histories that fit their belief, or selectively viewed the case histories to find evidence supporting their position. Still, they may be partially correct. It is possible that, in some instances, people have been creative, in part, due to mania and/or depression.

On the Other Hand

On the other hand, creativity often involves high level thinking, which seems like it would be impeded by any kind of mental disturbance. In fact, much of creativity seems to involve superior thinking, not distorted thinking (Boden 1990; Runco 1991). In my study of prisoners, the most creative were the conduct disorders, not the psychotics (Eisenman 1992a). In a study of the effects of mental illness and physical illness on creativity, both had negative, not positive effects (Eisenman 1990). From my work with schizophrenics, I have found that they prefer simple polygons, like noncreative people do (Eisenman 1991a), so I was surprised that Livesay (1984) predicted that schizophrenics would be higher in cognitive complexity than people without thought disorder. I was not surprised that he found that his schizophrenics were significantly less cognitively complex than the non-schizophrenics. "Mental illness" is a vague concept, usually referring to the most serious of the mental disorders: schizophrenia, bipolar disorder (manic-depression), or psychotic depression. Other mental disorders, such as obsessive-compulsive disorder or anxiety disorder are probably sometimes considered "mental illness" but usually are not. They, too, however, would seem to have a harmful effect on the clear, original thinking which is demanded for creativity.

Regression in the Service of the Ego:
A Psychoanalytic Perspective

A concept that might help tie together some of the conflicting findings regarding creativity and mental illness is that of Kris

(1952), regression in the service of the ego. Writing from a psychoanalytic perspective, Kris says that creative work may occur when the person regresses, but in the service of the ego, not the id. Regression in the service of the id (defined as the instinctual drives, such as sex and aggression) would be a totally irrational process and akin to psychosis or psychotic-like behavior. Any kind of regression has something in common with the non-normal nature of psychosis, but if the regression were truly in the service of the ego, it would be a regression in which there was both some loss of control and some subsequent control. Thus, insights gained during the regression, which here would likely refer to wild, primary-process thinking (as opposed to the normal, every-day rational secondary process thinking), could be utilized during the more rational post-regression stage. Or, perhaps, even during regression, if it were in the service of the ego, the person could utilize the irrational thinking in some useful fashion, and come up with a more creative outlook or invent an original and useful product.

Problems with Psychoanalytic Theory

The psychoanalytic language is very abstract, which is one of my objections to this theory. There really is nothing that is the id, or the ego, or even the superego. Nor are there any concrete things which could be designated primary or secondary process. All these things are abstractions, and if they help us understand things better then they are useful. But psychoanalysis often misleads, because we think we understand things when we use their abstract terms, when we might be better off studying the behavior of humans, their brain functioning, and other things which are more objective. People follow Freud and psychoanalysis as if it is a religion, utilizing the terms and thinking of everything in those terms. This holds us back from understanding things, although at times the psychoanalytic insights are good. Often, however, they need to be translated into more operational terms if they are to have scientific usefulness. These criticisms seem particularly true for psychoanalysis and its highly abstract language system, but they can be made for all fields, which tend to have their own parochial way of looking at things. For example, behaviorism has been just as dogmatic as psychoanalysis, although the value of behaviorism is that in attempting to tie things down to observable behavior, it allows for a more objective, scientific understanding, in which hypotheses can be tested and supported or rejected. Theories can be assessed via scientific investigations involving the collection of data. These theories can then be supported or falsified (Bernard 1990; Kuhn 1970; Popper 1968). Imagine trying to falsify "the id," or the psychoanalytic concept of the mind as composed of the id, ego, and superego, with the id and the superego as warriors fighting each other, and the ego as a conscious executive mediator. These concepts are so abstract it would be almost impossible to operationalize them for testing, and if you did succeed in operationalizing them, psychoanalysts would say, "That is not what we mean by our concepts."

At least the Kris (1952) conception of regression in the service of the ego is an advance over Freud's idea that creativity is entirely unconscious, based on motives which the creative person has not a clue about (Freud, 1916/1964). Freud's view seems to me to be overly neglecting of conscious thinking and in-control behaviors. Creative people often know what they are doing and have some high degree of conscious control (as well as being influenced by things they are not aware of). However, both views appeal to concepts difficult to test, unless operationalized in a way which most psychoanalysts would say destroys their integrity. Yet, ironically, these same psychoanalysts will often insist that psychoanalysis is a science. It is certainly not a science in the sense of what most of us who do research think a science is: testing hypotheses, testing theories, operationalizing concepts, supporting or falsifying theories, etc. At best, psychoanalysis, if a science at all, is a science in its most primitive stage, has remained so for many years, and most of its practitioners show little or no desire to advance beyond the abstract concepts which rule it. This is not to say that psychoanalysis cannot have interesting ideas, or useful insights for psychotherapy. It is to say that it remains mired in itself and will make limited contributions to advancing our knowledge about creativity or anything else, since it will always be limited by its metaphors and terminology. Again, this is true in general of any theory or school, but seems particularly a problem for psychoanalysis. This is not to say that psychoanalysis is incapable of contributing to our understanding of creativity. There have been some interesting psychoanalytic writings about creativity (Arieti 1976; Rosner and Abt 1974; Rothenberg 1979).

Psychoanalysis is really at least three things: a theory, which is what I have been discussing; a kind of psychotherapy; and, a method of investigation, such as using free association to get at what the subject thinks. This use of psychoanalysis as a method—free association or interpretation of dreams, to take two examples—could be where important contributions to creativity research could be made. Psychoanalysts, following Freud, typically do not gather quantifiable data to test ideas about their theories. But someone could, or could avoid testing the validity of psychoanalytic concepts and simply use some of the methods as an aid in understanding. I think they have a great deal of utility for research, which has been underutilized. Incidentally, for a stinging critique of psychoanalysis, far more negative than my position, see Eysenck (1992).

Mental Illness and Creativity

In the introduction, I suggested that (a) hypomania rather than the full-blown manic-depressive disorder may be most associated with creativity and (b) that already talented people may be the most helped to increase their creativity via hypomania. Richards and Kinney (1990) found support for (a) in that the milder mood swings were tied more closely to the enhancement of creativity than more extreme mood swings. However, for (b), they found that mild mood swings can enhance the creativity not only of eminent people but for what they call everyday creativity (Cropley 1990; Richards 1990; Richards and Kinney 1990; Richards, Kinney, Benet, and Merzel 1988; Richards, Kinney, Lund, Benet, and Merzel 1988). Thus, Richards and Kinney (1990) extend the findings of Andreasen (1987) with unipolar depressed writers and Jamison (1989) with British artists and writers. Both Andreasen and Jamison showed the importance for enhancing creativity of mood alteration, even where the alteration would be considered a mood disorder (Andreasen and Glick 1988; Jamison, Gerner, Harnmen, and Padesky 1980).

Subclinical "Disorder"

Schuldberg (1990) makes an important point. Instead of thinking of creativity or psychopathology as representing categories where you either have it or you do not, it is better to conceptualize both of them as continua. Thus, he is able to show that having schizotypal as well as hypomanic traits can enhance creativity. Schizotypal traits are those which have much in common with schizophrenia, but are not full-blown schizophrenia. My objection to linking schizophrenia with creativity has been that the true schizophrenic is so out of it and unable to control thinking or affect, that I do not see how this could be associated with creativity. Schuldberg (1990) suggests that having schizotypal traits might enhance creativity, and thus subclinical as opposed to a full-blown schizophrenic disorder would relate positively to creativity. For example, one of the major deficits of schizophrenics is their thought disorder, which is often manifested in the loose associations of schizophrenics. You say one word, or they think of an idea, and that brings about a whole train of associations which seem to cause the schizophrenic to now think of something totally different, and be unable to follow the original idea. This does not seem like it would relate to creativity, since schizophrenics cannot control their associative process. Hence, my skepticism about thinking that schizophrenia could be related to creativity. However, Schuldberg suggests that it is the schizophrenic's flight of ideas and not his/her loose associations which facilitate creativity.

A normal person having a flight of ideas (but not overly loose associations like a schizophrenic) could have a greater chance of being creative. Even loose associations could facilitate creativity if the person had some control over them. The schizophrenic seems not to, and thus is not creative. But, if the person had both loose associations but also some control, such as ego strength as discussed by Barron (1953) and Frank (1967), the person might be able to utilize his/her "pathology" for productive purposes (Schuldberg 1990; Strauss, Rakfeldt, Harding, and Lieberman 1989).

The Brain

It may be that creativity can be facilitated by brain processes, which we usually think of in negative terms, including the production of mental illness. I now believe that the major mental illnesses are largely brain disorders, as opposed to the environmental/learning explanations, which psychologists have tended to favor in recent times. Also, even some of the lesser mental disorders, such as obsessive-compulsiveness, may be due to genetic or biochemical processes, more so than to learning.

Mental Illness in a Friend

Part of my education on this matter occurred when a friend of mine called me on the telephone. She was in her late thirties, and worked only part time as a writer. Although she was one of the most intellectually perceptive, mentally healthy people I knew, from her words over the telephone I could tell that she was now a manic-depressive. The day before she seemed normal; today she had a bipolar disorder, with lots of manic speech patterns, such as rapidly going from one idea to another, with much of it not making much sense. Besides feeling terrible that this had happened to a friend of mine, I thought about what it meant. One day normal, the next day psychotic: this hardly seems like something produced by environmental factors, but was more consistent with a biochemical disorder.

Our bodies send messages to the brain via chemical and electrical impulses. If things get messed up, all kinds of strange things can happen, including, under certain circumstances, what we call psychosis. A similar thing happened to my niece when she developed diabetes, which is clearly not a learned disorder. One day she was fine, the next day she needed to drink excessive amounts of water and eat large quantities of food. Her body chemistry had changed. Her eating and drinking reflected the physiological needs that were now present in her pathological condition—diabetes.

There is a happy ending, of sorts, regarding my friend. Although she was violent and required brief hospitalization, she is now under control via lithium, which seems to work wonders in helping manic-depressives control their illness. She founded a support group for people with depression or manic-depression. In addition to spending time on that, she continued her writing and also worked with her support group to help people who have suffered as she did. Recently, she got an advanced degree and is now working with the mentally ill in her new job. The only negative side, besides having to take lithium for the rest of one's life (and the side effects, such as weight gain which lithium salt induces), is that she seems to have occasional fears or phobias, which seem to be carry overs from her disorder. For example, at times she is too terrified to ride on a train. It may be that one does not totally overcome psychosis, but carries, forever, some residual effects.

The Resistance of Psychologists

Psychologists are often resistant to thinking that the psychoses may develop much like any other physical illness, because this view tends to give greater power to psychiatrists and other medical doctors, whose training involves a greater understanding of physiology and brain pathology than almost all psychologists. Non-psychologists may also be taken in by our overemphasis on environmental causes of things, such as learning harmful ideas or behaviors. While many things can be explained environmentally, there may be many other important human behaviors which are better explained (or at least partially explained) in terms of genetics, physiology, the brain, and so forth. For example, while most research seems to link manic-depression not schizophrenia to creativity, some findings have shown that relatives of schizophrenics are higher in creativity than people who are not related to a schizophrenic (Heston 1966, Karlsson 1968, 1978; McNeil 1971). One way to explain this is to say that (a) schizophrenia is, at least in part, a genetic disorder and (b) the relatives of the schizophrenics also inherit something unusual, but in their case instead of inducing a full-blown schizophrenic illness, this inherited "something" enhances creativity.

Suggested Brain, Biochemical, and Genetic Effects

If the brain and biochemistry play an important role in creativity, what is it? We do not know, but there have been some suggestions. It may be that changes in the body and/or brain which cause harmful things, e.g. mental illness, can also produce helpful things which facilitate creativity. Prentky (1979, 1980, 1989) has discussed some of these kinds of things in detail, citing everything from research on humans to work with monkeys. The latter kind of research can show how damage to certain parts of the brain affects the ability of the animal, such as bilateral amygdalectomy causing decreased Galvanic Skin Response (GSR) to both pure and novel tones (Bagshaw, Kimble, and Pribam 1965), or a hippocampelectomy causing animals to act as if they cannot demonstrate internal inhibition (Kimble 1968).

On the human level, much of the work is speculative, since we cannot go around damaging the brains of human subjects to map out what brain area relates to what kind of behavior (although research can be ethically done on people who have suffered a particular kind of brain injury). Hoppe (1988) suggested that certain brain functioning, which increases emotionality, might increase creativity. Also, brain pathology could enhance creativity if it leads to mental illness, which in turn results in decreased social inhibitions and increased motivation and imagination (Ludwig 1989). Also, it may be that certain brain processes which facilitate the occurrence of mental illness also facilitate the occurrence of creativity (Miller 1988), or that the same gene which produces manic-depression or other pathology also produces creativity. If that is the case, it would explain, at least in part, the positive relationship between mental illness and creativity which recent research supports (Rushton 1990). Also, some things which are explainable at the brain level are also explainable at the environmental level as well. I think of the concept of arousability. While much of brain function is related to arousability, arousability can also be induced environmentally, and we know it to have an effect on creativity and probably intelligence as well (Martindale and Greenough 1973).

We need to know the specifics, which will only be found by more scientific research. Some hints are that affective disorder, especially bipolar disorder, seems related to creativity, but schizophrenia was not found to be related to creativity (Andreasen 1987; Soueif and Farag 1971; although, see the studies mentioned above about relatives of schizophrenics), and that creativity was highest when the bipolar disorder was under good control (Andreasen and Glick 1988). The creativity and mental illness of many eminent people supports the notion of a link between creativity and madness, at least in some instances (Bower 1989; Hershman and Lieb 1988; Holden, 1986). Creativity is, by definition, deviant (Eisenman 1991a). Perhaps whatever produces the creative deviance also produces, in some instances, mental illness or disorder.

The Concept of Deviance

A major advance in our understanding a lot of things—including creativity or mental illness—would occur if we used the concept of deviance. As I point out in my deviance book (Eisenman 1991a), deviance is a concept used by some sociologists and almost no psychologists. Psychologists talk about specific things, such as schizophrenia or drug abuse, but seldom bring a deviance perspective to bear on it. On the other hand, sociologists have somewhat of an advantage in that they use the concept of deviance to explain things in a non-obvious fashion. But, I say pox on the sociologists, too, since they almost always use deviance to indicate that something is bad, such as crime, where most of the deviance research occurs. But, deviance can be good: creativity, independence of judgment, the person in the lynch mob who says, "This is wrong," etc.

For creativity, mental illness, and other concepts, deviance is a useful concept because it makes us focus on how the person came to be defined as deviant. Thus, deviance is often based on social definition. Jan is defined as a drug abuser and so treated by society and may go to prison, be forced into psychotherapy, kicked out of the apartment by an angry manager, etc.; while Kelly who does the same things with regard to drugs is not so defined, and does not suffer the horrible consequences which befall Jan. Kelly's self-esteem is thus higher than Jan's, given what Jan has to go through.

One approach to deviance, the social labeling school, holds that deviance is nothing more than the successful application of the deviance label. Like many theories, this contains some wisdom but goes too far, Having worked with the mentally ill, I believe that they are typically disturbed, and not simply because someone labels them mentally ill. Having worked with prisoners, I believe they are usually antisocial people with no remorse for the horrible things they do, again not simply because they have been labeled as criminals. However, the labeling can make things worse, and thus the social labeling approach has some utility. Especially in emotional areas such as sex or drugs, a person's deviance may be little more than the social label attached to something he/she did which many others, perhaps most, also do (Eisenman 1991a, in press).

To be creative is, by definition, to be deviant, with deviance defined as meaning "different." Creative people will often engage in behavior which others disapprove of. Their creative behavior is already disapproved of by many members of conventional society, and it is easy for creative people, given their disregard for social convention and their risk-taking proclivities, to engage in other conduct which society condemns. This is how I view my research findings that creativity and illicit drug usage are positively correlated (Eisenman 1991a; Eisenman, Grossman and Goldstein 1980; Grossman, Goldstein, and Eisenman 1974; Victor, Grossman, and Eisenman 1973).

However, an interesting alternative interpretation is provided by Martindale (1989). Although he does not use the concept of deviance, he sees drug usage, including alcohol, as part of the creative process, in that psychopathology and creativity often go hand in hand. I have stressed that my findings are correlational and that I am not saying that drug usage causes creativity. But Martindale (1989) seems to be saying that drug usage can be part of psychopathology, which may be part of the same process as creativity. Although he never comes right out and says it, it appears to me that Martindale is saying that drug usage may be part of the cause of creative behavior. Whether cause or correlation, drug usage has been found to be related to creativity, and if we continue our national War on Drugs policy, with its attendant criminal prosecution as well as propaganda against all drug users, we will continue to lock up and persecute some of our most creative people (Eisenman in press).

From Creative, Deviant Movements to Conventional Oppressor: A Look at Psychoanalysis and Women's Liberation/Feminism

As a clinical psychologist who has done psychotherapy, I look to help clients achieve growth. This often involves overcoming the old, inhibited ways of doing things, and coming up with new, original (at least for the client) approaches. Criminals are an exception to being less inhibited; they often need to be more inhibited (Eisenman 1991a, 1991b). Social movements are like clients in some ways, and what is interesting is that social movements that were once creative often become stale and oppressive. Thus, the movement was for change and reform, but eventually becomes part of the repressive establishment. I recall a politician who told my father about the reform group that ousted him. "They said we were crooks, and that it was time for a change. Now they are as big a crooks as we were." I see two movements that started out as creative, innovative approaches, and which now show some signs of being less creative and more repressive. I believe a discussion of this is instructive, in that deviant (nonconforming) behavior may change and become repressively non-deviant, and possibly even worse than what the movement was trying to correct (e.g., the excesses of the French Revolution: "Off with their heads"). I discuss two important social movements, psychoanalysis and women's liberation/feminism as examples. It is worthwhile to analyze social movements, both to understand them better and for implications which the analysis may have for the behavior of individuals who also often fear freedom and retreat from it.

Psychoanalysis

I have already given my critique of psychoanalysis as a science. Here, I am concerned with how it may have been creative at one time and turned against that—at least to an extent.

Freud's invention of psychoanalysis was a major accomplishment. Growing up in the Victorian era, when people thought that behavior was rationally governed, Freud advanced the idea that motivation is primarily unconscious, often due to dark urges of sex and aggression. Freud was, therefore, an anti-rationalist; not in the sense that he did not use reason, but in the sense that he said reason does not form the major basis of human behavior. From Freud's ideas grew a theory; a new kind of psychotherapy (psychoanalysis); and a method of investigation, such as dream analysis and free association. Freud was no doubt wrong on many of his ideas, but his new kind of thinking was liberating—from seeing that sex was more important than people gave it credit for to seeing that people may have hidden motives in the joke they are telling, e.g., the joke may reveal hostility which the person could not otherwise express. Also, I believe that he was right to say that symbols, especially in dreams, are important and this was another important advance. However, his belief in universal symbols (symbol X always means Y) seems to me to be incorrect.

Freud helped overcome some of the Victorian repressiveness with his new ideas. Much of what he thought has been incorporated into our culture, so that laymen are Freudians, even if they do not know it. The Freudian ideas permeate everything from mass culture to serious writing, and most people who have not studied psychology know no other approach. Even professional advertisers know many of Freud's ideas, assume they are true, and try to incorporate them into the advertisements they produce.

This once liberating, anti-Victorian ideology is, however, often used for repressive purposes. Here are some of the things I have actually heard psychoanalysts saying, based on their theory.

1. *A man has several sexual partners.* This, they often conclude, shows repressed homosexuality, and is thus, by definition, deviant in the negative sense of "deviant" (Eisenman 1991a). The psychoanalytic concept here is that the man is engaged in a homosexual panic, defined as realizing, at some level, that he has homosexual tendencies. This induces a panic because he is opposed to homosexuality, so he engages in frequent heterosexual behaviors, with many partners, to reassure himself that he is not a homosexual. I once saw an example of this in a patient in a state mental hospital where I did my psychology internship. However, psychoanalysts, and those who follow the doctrine, make the mistake of applying what is probably a one in a thousand occurrence across the board to all men.

2. *A woman is capable of multiple orgasms.* We now know this to be a physiological reality. Whereas a man, after orgasm, undergoes a period of time, known as the refractory stage, wherein he cannot become sexually aroused, but a woman is capable of continual sexual arousal, and thus continual orgasms. Let us say that the woman induces multiple orgasms by allowing the water from the faucet of her tub to fall onto her clitoris and vaginal area. This shows penis envy, according to what some psychoanalysts have said, and indicates there is something wrong with her. Again, the person who is different in any way is put down as disturbed, even though in this example the person is functioning in what is a physiologically normal way to give herself pleasure.

3. *Students protest the policies of their university administration.* According to some psychoanalysts, these students have failed to resolve the Oedipus complex adequately. The university is the father, and they are rebelling against it because they unconsciously want to overthrow their father and sexually possess their mother. This far-fetched analysis fails to consider that there may be policies which are harmful and are worth protesting against. Is all protest to be explained in terms of some unconscious problem? This is reductionism at its worst: reducing whatever is observed to some other process, in this in stance a negative one. So there is a built in conservatism to this kind of

psychoanalytic doctrine. Anyone who works to achieve change is condemned.

4. *A person strongly disagrees with a psychoanalyst about something.* The analyst concludes that the strength of the disagreement shows that the person truly (though perhaps unconsciously) agrees, and is threatened by what the psychoanalyst has said. In this instance, you either agree with the psychoanalyst or your disagreement will be interpreted to his benefit. Either way, his position is unassailable, under the rules he has constructed.

5. *A woman has sex with more than one man, and is said by the psychoanalysts to be engaging in sexual acting out.* "Sexual acting out" is a somewhat vague concept, as I have pointed out (Eisenman 1987b, in press). It tends to refer to the person dealing with a problem by not facing that problem, but by engaging in sexual behavior instead. I found that the concept was applied more to women than to men, which is in accord with our sexual double standard, prohibiting behaviors in women that are allowable for men (Eisenman 1987b, 1991a, in press). This cultural standard has its effect since females, on the average, engage in less sexual behavior than do male (Eisenman 1982), no doubt in part because society makes them feel like they are bad if they do certain things which are, however, not prohibited, or less prohibited for males (Eisenman 1991a).

The above examples all show psychoanalysis at its worse. One might defend the movement by saying that everyone makes errors, and that these are just some negative examples. But, the issue is, how likely are these kind of errors? I think they are very frequent, and show that psychoanalysis, at least as practiced by real-life psychoanalysts, has a repressive, anti-creativity spirit. Instead of allowing the person to grow, the person is put into some category which serves a traditional, conservative, repressive function. The person is labeled as some kind of deviant, in the bad sense of the word (which is, unfortunately, how most people think of "deviance"), and his/her behavior is thus explained away as being based on some underlying pathology.

Women's Liberation/Feminism

Originally, the feminist movement was called women's liberation. The name change is very interesting. "Women's liberation" was a radical movement, suggesting major changes in the way women are viewed and live their lives. In 1972–73, I was a visiting associate professor at the University of California at Santa Cruz. The woman's liberation movement, sometimes also referred to as feminism back then, was a powerful, creative movement, which suggested that women were being kept down in their role as housewives, and that life should entail more than taking care of a house and raising children. Women should have equality in the workplace, in the bedroom, and in general. Sexual freedom was a major part of the women's movement as I observed it then, and women opposed the game-playing that goes on in male-female relationships. Sex roles can, of course, be very confining (Cyrus 1993). They said that women's liberation would liberate men, too, and this seemed like an accurate statement. Greater sexual freedom for women and less conventional role playing would mean greater freedom for men. To demonstrate their freedom, many women's liberation advocates in California would go topless at rock music concerts, showing their freedom from oppressive rules and laws.

In later years, the term "women's liberation" was heard less and less, and was replaced by "feminism." It is less clear what feminism means per se. "Liberation" implies a radical change, while "feminism" seems to imply less. "Feminism" seems to imply the rights of women, without suggesting any need to be liberated from conventional standards.

In recent times, not only have many feminists seemed to drop their interest in liberation and sexual freedom, but they have become sexually repressive. Two major examples are (1) the feminist condemnation of pornography and the attempt to show that it is a major cause of rape, and (2) the feminist emphasis on sexual harassment.

With regard to the pornography issue, the feminists seem to be thinking in shallow terms. Rapists are not primarily motivated by pornography, if at all. There may be individual case histories where rapists read pornography before committing a crime, but that does not mean that if there had been no pornography there would be no rape. In fact, from working with rapists and reading the research literature, many rapists come from repressive, harsh backgrounds where learning about sex, or reading about it, or looking at pictures of it is taboo. The best research on this was the comprehensive investigation by the Committee on Obscenity and Pornography (1970), which had vast resources, and concluded that pornography had little or no effect on behavior.

Also, the issue of what constitutes pornography is vague. Feminists usually include the relatively sanitized nudity of *Playboy* magazine within their definition of pornography, which is dubious. Gloria Steinem, a major feminist leader (with whom I usually agree), said that pornography is bad but that erotica is good. The trouble is, without a clear definition, pornography is the erotica she does not like, and erotica is the pornography she does like. American society is more puritanical and sexually repressed than many think (Eisenman 1991a). We may need more pornography, or at least more sexually explicit material, if we are to grow as a culture. I might exclude from this position pornography that combines female nudity with violence. This combination may be harmful, while I believe most other pornography to be mostly benign. The whole idea that nudity or sexuality is bad is a part of American values that needs to be overcome so that people will be liberated. If this were the case, then what we call pornography (including *Playboy*) would be no big deal, and would merely be seen as just another form of entertainment. Instead, today, with all our sexual inhibitions, we see pornography (or erotica; I use the terms interchangeably because I doubt that they can be differentiated) as Satanic.

Instead of pursuing sexual freedom, feminists seem out to get men, and take away some of their freedom. The concept of "sexual harassment" has been a way to prosecute and persecute men who fail to conform to some conservative standard of sexual behavior. Of course, it is important to note that true sexual harassment is horrible and has a devastating effect on the victims. But feminists have cast their net very wide, so that telling a dirty joke or having pin-up pictures on one's wall is seen as sexual harassment. Women claim they want men to be more honest and open, but if a man is honest with a women about his sexual interest in her, he leaves himself open for an accusation of sexual harassment, because he can be accused of making an unwanted sexual advance. Since it is often impossible to know if an advance is wanted or unwanted, this puts the man in the position of inhibiting his behavior if he wants to avoid possible charges. The result reminds me of a cartoon I once saw. A man and a woman pass each other on the street. You see what they are thinking. Each would like to approach the other, but fears being thought of negatively, so they pass by without speaking. On a network television news program, feminist Robin Morgan said that men can avoid harassing women by adhering to the following rule of thumb: "If you are not sure, don't do it." While this would certainly work to cut out offensive behavior, it would also work to eliminate any kind of risk taking or creative behavior. It is the advice of repression.

Feminists have largely won in the sexual harassment arena. Their position has become the law of the land, and it is easy to bring charges of sexual harassment and put the man on the defensive. Many organizations, fearing law suits, will side with the woman and punish the man, often with no hearing or with a kangaroo court type hearing, wherein the man is sure to be "convicted" so that the organization can say "See, we oppose sexual harassment."

At other times, though, women who bring charges are, themselves, persecuted, and the organization fails to deal with real, ongoing harassment. Rape in the military is an example of this according to a 1992 network news magazine broadcast. Many female soldiers are raped by the male soldiers, but they are not believed and further harassed by the military if they complain.

Few people have looked at the sexual harassment of males by females. This is not what feminists want, since their movement seems designed to help women and persecute men when wrong doing is alleged. It is interesting to see the knee-jerk fashion in which many feminists side with the alleged victim (female), when she makes a complaint against an alleged perpetrator (male). The feminists, without much factual knowledge, assume that the woman is telling the truth and that the man is guilty. Our study of sexual harassment

proclivities in both men and women found that the same variables which related to sexual harassment proclivities by men
also related to sexual harassment proclivities by women:
acceptance of traditional sex roles, belief in rape myths, and
other traditional, conservative beliefs (Bartling and Eisenman
in press). One conceptual problem is that while a female
recipient of some behavior might regard it as sexual harassment, the male recipient of the same behavior would often
not consider what was done to him to be sexual harassment.
Thus, females object to more behaviors than males object to.
In this sense, females are more conservative than males.

The assault on sexually explicit material and on male sexual behavior is an attempt to turn back the clock and make
men as inhibited as women used to be—and perhaps still are.
So, instead of trying to liberate themselves, feminists are, in
part, trying to unliberate men. It is thus a repressive, puritanical movement.

Why the Change?

Why has all of the above occurred? I do not know, although it
seems to be the way things often occur: a movement starts out
creative and risk taking and ends up repressive and conservative. However, I have come across an explanation of why it
occurs, and although I find this explanation disturbing and do
not want to believe it, it does provide an answer, so I will mention it. This explanation is what could be called the biological
explanation of Wilson (1992). He says that evolution has made
men and women very different. Some of the differences,
which he believes to be innate, are that women, relative to
men, are more submissive, less skilled in spatial or mathematical skills, less risk taking, but higher in empathy, verbal skills,
and social skills. Wilson believes these are biological truths,
not really subject to great change by culture. Thus, from this
perspective, women's liberation made a mistake in trying to
achieve sexual freedom and all the other kinds of freedom for
women, because women do not really want this, as it goes
against their nature. Thus, it is no surprise that the freedom of
the women's liberation movement has been toppled for the
puritanical repressiveness of the feminist movement. This, in
a nutshell, is the Wilson (1992) perspective on the feminist

movement. I do not like his biological determinism and its implication that things cannot change very much, but he does provide an explanation that explains the change from women's liberation to feminism. In fact, it is the only explanation I know of which specifically addresses that freedom-to-repression change.

I would prefer to believe that some of the ideals of the women's liberation movement can be recaptured and some of the excesses of the current feminist movement overcome. In fact, some feminists agree with my position, and do not support the assault on pornography, the simple-minded view that it is a main cause of rape, or the constant attempt to nail men on sexual harassment charges, or to verbally put them down when they do something such as telling an off color joke. Thus, some feminists have not been taken in by what appears to be the majority part, and there is hope that things could change. Biological views tend to have the implication that things really cannot change, and that the way things are is, more or less, the way things should be. Thus, they tend to support a conservative, traditional ideology which says that old ways are good ways, and let's not have all this change. If women are truly low in risk taking, for example, then there will always be a sex difference with men, on the average, being more creative than women, since risk taking is often part of being creative (Davis 1992; Eisenman 1969a, 1987a, 1991a; Merrifield, Guilford, Christensen, and Frick 1961; Pankove and Kogan 1968). On the other hand, if women are taught to avoid risk, then they can be taught to take risk, and there need not necessarily be a sex difference in creativity.

The feminist movement has had a powerful effect in helping women see that their potential is much more than what they have traditionally been taught. One need only to look at the letters-to-the-editor section of women's magazines to see that even fairly simple articles, about personal growth or job opportunities for women, result in letters saying things like "I never before realized that I had options in my life. This article was an incredible, eye-opening experience." Much credit for the expanded horizons for women goes to the women's liberation/feminist movement. It is tragic that the movement seems to be headed in a puritanical, repressive direction.

References

Andreasen, N. C. 1987. Creativity and mental illness: Prevalence rates in writers and the first-degree relatives. *American Journal of Psychiatry, 144,* 1288–1292.

———. Andreasen, N. C. and I. D. Glick. 1988. Bipolar affective disorder and creativity: Implication and clinical management. *Comprehensive Psychiatry, 29,* 207–217.

Arieti, S. 1976. *Creativity, the magic synthesis.* New York: Basic Books.

Bagshaw, M. H., D. P. Kimble, and K. H. Pribram. 1965. The GSR of monkeys during orienting and habituation and after ablation of the amygdala, hippocampus and inferotemporal cortex. *Neuropsychologia, 3,* 111–119.

Barron, F. 1953. An ego-strength scale which predicts response to psychotherapy. *Journal of Consulting Psychology, 5,* 327–333.

Bartling, C. A., and R. Eisenman. In press. Sexual harassment proclivities in men and women. *Bulletin of the Psychonomic Society.*

Bernard, T. J. 1990. Twenty years of testing theories: What have we learned and why? *Journal of Research in Crime and Delinquency, 27,* 325–347.

Boden, M. A. 1990. *The creative mind: Myths and mechanisms.* New York: Basic Books.

Bower, H. 1989. Beethoven's creative illness. *Australian and New Zealand Journal of Psychiatry, 23,* 111–116.

Committee on Obscenity and Pornography. 1970. *Report of the Commission on Obscenity and Pornography.* Washington, DC: U. S. Government Printing Office.

Cropley, A. J. 1990. Creativity and mental health in everyday life. *Creativity Research Journal, 3,* 167–178.

Cyrus, V. 1993. *Experiencing race, class, and gender in the United States.* Mountain View, CA: Mayfield.

Davis, G. A. 1992. *Creativity is forever* (3rd edit). Dubuque, IA: Kendall/Hunt.

Eisenman, R. 1969a. Components of creativity, verbal conditioning, and risk taking. *Perceptual and Motor Skills, 39,* 687–700.

———. 1969b. Creativity and mental illness: A prevalent stereotype. *Perceptual and Motor Skills, 29,* 34.

———. 1982. Sexual behavior as related to sex fantasies and experimental manipulation of authoritarianism and creativity. *Journal of Personality and Social Psychology, 43,* 853–860.

———. 1987a. Creativity, birth order, and risk taking. *Bulletin of the Psychonomic Society, 25,* 87–88.

———. 1987b. Sexual acting out: Diagnostic category or moral judgment? *Bulletin of the Psychonomic Society, 25,* 198–200.

———. 1990. Creativity, preference for complexity, and physical and mental illness. *Creativity Research Journal, 3,* 231–236.

———. 1991a. *From crime to creativity: Psychological and social factors in deviance.* Dubuque, IA: Kendall/Hunt.

———. 1991b. Monitoring and postconfinement treatment of sex offenders: An urgent need. *Psychological Reports, 69,* 1089–1090.

———. 1992a. Creativity in prisoners: Conduct disorders and psychotics. *Creativity Research Journal, 5,* 175–181.

———. 1992b . Living with a psychopathic personality: Case history of a successful anti-social personality. *Acta Paedopsychiatrica, 55,* 241–243.

———. In press. Creativity and impulsivity: The deviance perspective. In W. McCown, M. B. Shure, and J. Johnson, eds. *The impulsive client: Theory, research, and treatment.* Washington, DC: American Psychological Association.

———. R. Goldstein, and J. C. Grossman, Undergraduate marijuana use as related to internal sensation novelty seeking and openness to experience. *Journal of Clinical Psychology, 36,* 1013–1019.

Eysenck, H. J. 199. *The decline and fall of the Freudian empire.* Washington, DC: Scott-Townsend.

Frank, G. H. 1967. A review of research with measures of ego strength derived from the MMPI and the Rorschach. *Journal of General Psychology, 77,* 183–206.

Freud, S. 1964. *Leonardo da Vinci and a memory of his childhood.* New York: Norton. (Originally published 1916.)

Grinder, R. E. 1985. The gifted in our midst: By their divine deeds, neurosis, and mental test scores we have known them. In F. D. Horowitz and M. O'Brien, eds. *The gifted and talented: Developmental perspectives* (pp. 5–35). Washington, DC: American Psychological Association.

Grossman, J. C., R. Eisenman, and J. Goldstein. 1974. Openness to experience and marihuana use in college students. *Psychiatric Quarterly, 48,* 86–92.

Hershman, D. J., and J. Lieb. 1988. *The key to genius: Manic-depression and the creative life* Buffalo, NY: Prometheus Books.

Heston, L. L. 1966. Psychiatric disorders in foster home reared children of schizophrenic mothers. *British Journal of Psychiatry, 112,* 819–825.

Holden, C. 1986. Manic depression and creativity. *Science, 233,* 725.

Hoppe, K. D. 1988. Hemispheric specialization and creativity. *Psychiatric Clinics of North America, 11,* 303–315.

Jamison, K. R., 1989. Mood disorders and patterns of creativity in British writers and artists. *Psychiatry, 52,* 125–134,

Jamison, K. R., R. Gerner, C. Hammen, and C. Padesky. 1980. Clouds and silver linings: Positive experiences associated with primary affective disorders. *American Journal of Psychiatry, 137*, 198–202.

Karlsson, J. L. 1968. Genealogical studies of schizophrenia. In D. Rosenthal and S. S. Kety, eds. *The transmission of schizophrenia* (pp. 85–94). Oxford, England: Pergamon.

Karlsson, J. L. 1978. Inheritance of creative intelligence: A study of genetics in relation to giftedness and its implications for future generations. Chicago: Nelson-Hall.

Kimble, D. P. 1968. The hippocampus and internal inhibition. *Psychological Bulletin, 70* 285–295.

Kris, E. 1952. *Psychoanalytic explorations in art.* New York: International Universities Press

Kuhn, T. 1970. *The structure of scientific revolutions.* Chicago: University of Chicago Press.

Livesay, J. R. 1984. Cognitive complexity-simplicity and inconsistent interpersonal judgment in thought-disordered schizophrenia. *Psychological Reports, 54*, 759–768.

Ludwig, A. M. 1989. Reflections on-creativity and madness. *American Journal of Psycho therapy, 43*, 4–14.

Martindale, C. 1989. Personality, situation, and creativity. In J. A. Glover, R., C. R. Reynolds, and R. Ronning, eds. *Handbook of Creativity* (pp. 211–232). New York: Plenum.

Martindale, C., and J. Greenough. 1973. The differential effect of increased arousal on creative and intellectual performance. *Journal of Genetic Psychology, 123*, 329–335.

McNeil, T. F. 1971. Prebirth and postbirth influences on the relationship between creative ability and recorded mental illness. *Journal of Personality, 39*, 391–406.

Miller, L. 1988. Ego autonomy, creativity, and cognitive style: A neuropsychodynamic approach. *Psychiatric Clinics of North America, 11*, 383–397.

Popper, K. 1968. *The logic of scientific discovery.* New York: Harper and Row.

Prentky, R. A. 1979. Creativity and psychopathology: A neurocognitive perspective. In B. A. Maher, ed. *Progress in experimental personality research* (Vol. 9, pp. 1–39). New York: Academic Press.

———. 1980. Creativity and psychopathology: A neurocognitive perspective. New York: Praeger.

———. 1989. *Creativity and psychopathology: Gamboling at the seat of madness.* In J. A. Glover, C. R. Reynolds, and R. R. Ronning eds. Handbook of creativity (pp. 243–269). New York: Plenum.

Richards, R. 1990. Everyday creativity, eminent creativity, and health: "Afterview" for CRJ issues on creativity and health. *Creativity Research Journal, 3*, 300–326.

————. and D. K. Kinney. 1990. Mood swings and creativity. *Creativity Research Journal, 3*, 203–218.

————. M. Benet, D. K. Kinney, and A. P. C. Merzel. 1988. Assessing everyday creativity: Characteristics of The Lifetime Creativity Scales and validation with three large samples. *Journal of Personality and Social Psychology, 54*, 476–485.

————. 1988. Creativity in manic-depressives, cyclothymiacs, and their normal relatives, and control subjects. *Journal of Abnormal Psychology, 97*, 281–288.

Rosner, S., and L. E. Abt. 1974. *Essays in creativity.* Croton-on-Hudson, NY. North River Press.

Rothenberg, A. 1979. *The emerging goddess: The creative process in art, science, and other fields.* Chicago: University of Chicago Press.

————. 1990. Creativity, mental health, and alcoholism. *Creativity Research Journal, 3*, 179–201.

Runco, M. A., ed. 1991. *Divergent thinking.* Norwood, NJ: Ablex.

Rushton, J. P. 1990. Creativity, intelligence, and psychoticism. *Personality and Individual Differences, 11*, 1291–1298.

Schuldberg, D. 1990. Schizotypal and hypomanic traits, creativity, and physical health. *Creativity Research Journal, 3*, 218–230.

Soueif, M. I., and S. E. Farag. 1971. Creative thinking aptitude in schizophrenia: A factorial study. *Sciences de l'Art* (Paris), *8*, 51–60.

Strauss, J. S., J. Harding, P. Lieberman, and J. Rakfeldt. 1989. Psychological and social aspects of negative symptoms. *British Journal of Psychiatry, 155* (Suppl. 7), 128–132.

Victor, H. R., R. Eisenman, and J. C. Grossman. Openness to experience and marijuana use in high school students. *Journal of Consulting and Clinical Psychology, 41*, 78–85.

Wallace, D. B. 1985. Giftedness and the construction of a creative life. In F. D. Horowitz and M. O'Brien, eds. *The gifted and talented: Developmental perspectives* (pp. 361–385). Washington, DC: American Psychological Association.

————. 1989. Studying the individual: The case study method and other genres. *Archives de Psychologie, 57*, 69–90.

Wilson, G. 1992. *The great sex divide.* Washington, DC: Scott-Townsend.

Zigler, E., and E. A. Farber. 1985. Commonalities between the intellectual extremes: Giftedness and mental retardation In F. D. Horowitz and M. O'Brien, eds. *The gifted and talented: Developmental perspectives* (pp. 387–408). Washington, DC: American Psychological Association.

Conservative Sexual Values: Effects of an Abstinence Program on Student Attitudes

There are many important differences between liberals vs. conservatives (Eisenman 1991b; Eisenman and Cole 1964; Eisenman and Sirgo 1991, 1992; Sirgo and Eisenman, 1990, in press). Conservatives tend to value order and individual responsibility and control, while liberals are more likely to value variety and personal freedom. Further, conservatives tend to want the government to stay out of their business except to assist at times, and to maintain order (Cuniff 1993; Fuelner 1993). The removal of government controls from the economy is seen by conservatives as allowing capitalism to work and make for a wealthier society, with a higher standard of living, including improved health through better nutrition, technology, medicine, etc. (Gold 1992). However, there is one area where conservatives tend to want government interference in order to produce more order and control. That is in the area of sexual behavior. Many conservatives see sexual freedom as an evil, which can lead to the decline of the society. Anti-drug attitudes also show this paradox, with conservatives wanting more government interference. One of the ways in which conservatives have tried to get their sexual values enforced is via school classes on abstinence. Just as there has been a "Just Say No to Drugs" movement, so, too, is there a "Just Say No to Sex" movement, although it does not so describe itself.

The present study is an analysis of data made available by a publisher of educational materials, which puts out a curriculum program attempting to get students to refrain from intercourse before marriage. A sexuality curriculum is made available to schools, but the emphasis is on how to avoid intercourse before marriage. Students are taught how to stand up to peer-group pressure to engage in sex, and to think of abstinence as reflecting the real sexual freedom, etc. Would such an approach work with today's students, who are constantly exposed to sexual stimulation in the media and from their own peer group? The present study provides a statistical analysis of the data from the educational materials organization to see if their approach can change student attitudes in the direction they wished.

Method

Subjects

The participants were 1800 students in grades 7–10 in four states: Illinois, Kansas, Missouri, and Wisconsin.

Procedure

The students were provided with materials from *Sex Respect*, a publication designed to teach conservative attitudes toward premarital sexuality and to teach students how to avoid peer group pressure for sex, how to see abstinence as the true sexual freedom, how to care for another without sexual intercourse, and other similar teachings (Mast 1990). The materials make up the curriculum for a class in sexuality, and include written material and videos promoting the message. In addition to the students having booklets, which emphasize the different messages, the teachers and parents have similar instructional material, guiding them in working with the students. The students answered a questionnaire, pre- and post-class, on sexual attitudes.

Results

All statistical results are two-tailed binomial tests, based on whether the student attitude increased or decreased from pre- to post-testing, i.e. from before the course vs. after the instruction was completed. Before the course 20% of the students said that they thought that sexual urges are controllable, vs. 30% saying they are controllable after the course ($p < .001$).

Before the course 12% thought that television and movies influenced a great deal what they did on a date vs. 31% who thought this after the course ($p < .00 1$). Is the sex act wrong for unmarried teenagers if no pregnancy occurs? Before the course 36% said "yes" vs. 66% after the course ($p < .001$). Are there a lot of benefits to waiting until marriage to have sexual intercourse? Before the course 35% said "yes," while after the course 58% said "yes" ($p < .001$).

Discussion

The results clearly showed that attitudes were changed in the direction desired by the curriculum publishers, i.e., in the direction of more sexually conservative values. These values are, however, statements of belief. The next step would be to see if the students really change their behavior in accord with what they profess to now believe. It may be that some do and some do not, in which case it would be useful to know what variables distinguish between those who actually do inhibit their behavior as opposed to those who comply verbally, but not behaviorally.

Education is usually predicated upon informing people of the different views available (Aronson 1988; Husen and Postlethwaite 1985), while the curriculum discussed here is, in some ways, perhaps better thought of as being persuasion or propaganda. The distinction between education and propaganda can be subtle, but education imparts knowledge or skill, while propaganda presents one doctrine (Aronson 1988). The curriculum studied here does both: it provides a great deal of information, but it is done in the context of a conservative doctrine about sex.

Sex is often an emotional topic on which people have contradictory beliefs (Eisenman 1991a). Schools have instituted sex education courses for a variety of reasons: to help people understand sexuality, to fight the AIDS crisis, and to help prevent teenage pregnancy. Some writers have debated whether or not sex education provides sufficient moral guidance (Ryan 1991; Scales 1991). The present study shows that a conservative moral orientation can lead to an outcome in accord with the conservative sexual values, at least as far as questionnaire responses are concerned. Whether this is a proper curriculum and whether (or to what extent) it exerts behavioral change is another issue entirely.

References

Aronson, E. 1988. *The social animal* (5th edit.). New York: Freeman.

Cuniff, J. 1993, Jan. 6. Conservatives angry at Bush, business by executives. *Lake Charles American Press,* p. 4.

Eisenman, R. 1991a. *From crime to creativity: Psychological and social factors in deviance.* Dubuque, IA: Kendall/Hunt.

————. 1991b. Gender and racial prejudice of conservative college women. *Psychological Reports, 68,* 450.

————. and S. N. Cole. 1964. Prejudice and conservatism in denominational college students. *Psychological Reports, 14,* 644.

————. and H. B. Sirgo. 1991. Liberals versus conservatives: Personality, child-rearing attitudes, and birth order/sex differences. *Bulletin of the Psychonomic Society, 29,* 240–242.

————. and H. B. Sirgo. 1992, March. *Racial attitudes and voting behavior in the 1988 national elections.* Paper presented at the Southwestern Social Science Association annual meeting, Austin, TX.

Fuelner, E. J., Jr. 1993. *State of conservatism.* Washington, DC: The Heritage Foundation.

Gold, S. 1992, November. The rise of markets and the fall of infectious disease. *The Freeman, 42* (11), 412–415.

Husen, T., and T. N. Postlethwaite, eds. 1985. *The international encyclopedia of education.* New York and London: Pergamon.

Mast, C. K. 1990. *Sex Respect: The option of true sexual freedom.* Topeka, KS: Temco.

Ryan, K. 1991. Sex, morals, and schools. In J. W. Noll (ed.), *Taking sides: Clashing views on controversial educational issues.* (pp. 330–335). Guilford, CT: Dushkin.

Scales, P. 1991. Overcoming future barriers to sexuality education. In J. W. Noll, ed. *Taking sides: Clashing views on controversial educational issues* (pp. 336–342). Guilford, CT: Dushkin.

Sirgo, H. B., and R. Eisenman. 1990. Perception of governmental fairness by liberals and conservatives. *Psychological Reports, 67,* 1331–1334.

————. In press. Liberals versus conservatives: Are attitudes toward government related to experiences with government? *Bulletin of the Psychonomic Society.*

School-Sanctioned Violence Against Children

XOX XOX XOX XOX XOX XOX XOX XOX XOX XOX XOX XOX XOX XOX

A very moving television show on corporal punishment was shown on a program called "The West." It showed what looked like the severely bruised buttocks of very small children who had suffered school-sanctioned corporal punishment. It also presented the case of a child of about eight-years old who planned to kill himself after receiving corporal punishment in the school. Among other things, the corporal punishment made him feel like a failure. Many school districts allow the corporal punishment of children as proper discipline for misdeeds. These districts have a legal mandate to inflict what should be called beatings on the children. The misdeeds may be serious, but at times children are paddled for missing classes, even if they were sick. Parents and school administrators sometimes justify this physical attack on children with an appeal to the Bible: *Spare the rod and spoil the child.* Others think it necessary for the school to have control over the pupils. However, I reflected that corporal punishment is not the only way in which schools sanction violence against children

My Grammar School Experiences

I recall a horrible incident when I was in grammar school, which has remained with me still. I was in about the seventh grade and we went to a park with the teacher for recess. One kid punched another in the stomach, and the kid vomited. A child went up to the teacher and said, very excitedly, "Miss Jones, Billy Tayor punched Tom Wilson in the stomach and made him sick." The teacher said "Yeah, okay," and did absolutely nothing about it. This made me realize that I was a potential victim and that the teacher would do nothing to protect me. Incidentally, this teacher could be moved to action, but not, apparently, because of physical violence. When I wanted to listen to the baseball World Series on a portable radio, instead of playing softball with the rest of the kids, she was furious and yelled at me "Who do you think you are? Do you think you are better than everyone else?" and similar things. She made me conform to playing softball, like everyone else.

Experiences of a Colleague

A colleague of mine reports a similar experience, which also reflects school-sanctioned violence against children. He was often beat up at school by other kids and the school did nothing about it. He recalls thinking about his experiences with the bullies: "If I were an adult, they would be arrested for assault and battery, but since I am a kid, nothing is done." Thus, the school allowed violence against a child to occur.

Are Schools Opposed to Violence?

The above examples involve the school not doing enough to stop violence, while corporal punishment involves the school taking an active role in administering violence. It seems that our schools are not always opposed to violence against children, nor do they always protect the children entrusted to their care. The indifference to violence reported here may be consistent with the use of corporal punishment in many school districts. The consistency is a disregard for the physical welfare of the child. In one case the child is not protected against violence by other children, and in the other instance the child is the victim of violence by the school, via the administration of corporal punishment. Thus, while school officials may complain of things such as gang violence in their schools, these same officials may be supporting violence against children, either through neglect, or via the direct administration of physical punishment in districts where that is allowed. It is curious that the school culture actually encourages violence at the same time that violence is condemned. Somehow, the school's imposition of physical violence is neither seen as violence nor as wrong. Also, the failure to protect children from violence is often due to teachers or administrators who do not have the skills or the empathy to help vulnerable children avoid harm at the hands of others.

Gangs

XOX XOX XOX XOX XOX XOX XOX XOX XOX XOX XOX XOX XOX XOX

When I was Senior Clinical Psychologist in a prison treatment program for youthful male offenders, I worked with gang members. Most of the gang members were from the greater Los Angeles area, since ours was a state prison which took in prisoners from southern and central California. Los Angeles has large numbers of gang members, typically Hispanic or black. There are a few white gangs, such as the Skinheads who are racist and enjoy being violent. I wish to describe what gang members are like, so that people will have a greater understanding. Such improved understanding may help prevent the kind of mistake made in Lake Charles, Louisiana where a Los Angeles gang member was placed in an unlocked facility, and, of course escaped.

The main thing to realize about these youth gangs is that they place a high value on (a) being antisocial and committing crimes and (b) being violent. Many of the youth could be acceptable citizens if they could get away from the gang influence. But once they are in a gang, and as long as they remain gang members, their loyalty is to the gang. It does not matter if they are twelve or thirteen years old, they will be prepared to commit the most horrendous of crimes in support of the gang ideology.

Why Do They Join?

Why would anyone join such gangs? I think the answer is at least twofold. One: The gangs attract people who are already predisposed to be antisocial. Two: The horrible family backgrounds of many of the youths make a "family-like" organization attractive. The gang becomes their family, providing some support and obtaining loyalty in return. Most of the youth I worked with grew up in father-absent homes, in poverty, and had often been neglected, possibly abused (physically or sexually), and saw little about the future to make them believe they could succeed in the straight world.

The Solution

The only solution would be to get the youth out of the gangs and, preferably, out of their neighborhoods. If they return to the same neighborhood, the likelihood is high that they will return to antisocial behavior, probably with their gang. Thus, in my view, no matter how much counseling or therapy the youths receive, if something is not done to remove them from the environment, which fostered the behavior in the fist place, there is little hope for them becoming law-abiding citizens. The ideal approach would involve both treatment and environmental change. Some will still continue on their antisocial path no matter what we do, but others can be reached.

Chapter Sixteen

Life in the Penal Colony

XOX XOX XOX XOX XOX XOX XOX XOX XOX XOX XOX XOX XOX XOX

At times, I wondered why I had chosen to work in a prison. At one level of explanation, it was so that I could be in California, where all of my family had moved. But the job was certainly different from my university experiences. Sure, I had experienced unpleasant manipulations from students, trying to get a better grade or achieve some favor. However, the prisoners were real pros, and they used intimidation when they thought it necessary. They would seldom overtly threaten to hurt me, but the threat was often in the air.

It was Monday, and I had to attend a training session on prison security. It was explained to us that although the session might seem unrelated to our job, security was a very important issue and affected everyone. The speaker was an old-timer, a guard named Homer. "Convicts always give themselves away," he said. "They leave tracks in the snow," which got a laugh, since it was 75 degrees outside and seldom rained here in southern California, and certainly never snowed. But we knew what he meant. Anything we do leaves a trace of ourselves, in one way or another. I have forgotten most of what he said, but the phrase, "tracks in the snow," stuck with me.

On Tuesday, I ran my drug therapy group, composed of prisoners deemed by the parole board to have serious drug problems, which needed to be addressed and changed before the convicts could be granted parole. Amazingly, half the group insists that they have no drug problem. My job, in part, is to get them to see otherwise. Billy, a highly emotional eighteen-year old who often causes problems is at it again. Before the group even starts, he yells, "I don't see why I have to be in this stupid group. I told you before, I don't have a drug problem. And, even if I did, being in this group would be a waste of time. If I want to use drugs when I get out, I'll use them, and none of you can change that. It's up to me. So why waste my time by making me be here? It's stupid." I try to explain to him that something may happen in the group to make him change and to be of benefit to him, but he is having none of it. "I don't want anything to help me. If I want to do something, I will do it; and if I don't, I won't. It's as simple as that. Why don't you leave me alone. If I have to stay in this group, I will; but don't say anything to me." When I say, "Billy, why do you feel that way?" he says, "I told you not to say anything to me," and turns his head and body away from me.

I try to ignore Billy and start the session, hoping he will be drawn in later by me or by other members of the group. But he refuses to say anything and pretends not to hear us. When one of the other prisoners says, "Billy, why don't you participate? You are just like us. We all have drug problems," Billy gives the prisoner an angry look and says "Damn it, I said to leave me alone. Are you deaf or what?" The prisoner responds with hostility, obeying the unwritten prisoners' rule that you do not let another seem to intimidate you in any way. "Billy, you're a jerk. People are trying to help you." Billy, obeying the same "rule" says "You're a jerk. And, if you bother me anymore, you're going to be sorry."

I can feel a fight about to begin, so I say some things to calm them both down, such as "Let's not get angry at each other, but see how we can help each other, especially with regard to drug usage." I sense that Billy is not going to get much out of this group and that he will continue to be a disruptive force, so I ask him, "Billy, would you like to go back to your room?" and he responds affirmatively. I call the unit and ask them to send a guard over to remove one of the prisoners, but I am told "Everyone is busy now, can't you handle it?" This is an annoying question, since I would not have called if I did not need help. Also, it forces me to say into the phone, where everyone in the room can hear me, that things may be getting out of control. I communicate this without actually coming out and saying it, and they promise to send someone over soon. After about five minutes a guard appears and Billy is taken back to be locked in his room. But he has poisoned the atmosphere. The group does not go well. Some pick up his message about not needing help, or not wanting help, while others seem to be in a combative mood. He has left his tracks in the snow.

Home

I go home that night feeling unhappy about the poor drug therapy group session. I feel that little has been accomplished. Instead of being a group therapist, I was more like a referee. I try to think of previous group sessions that have gone well, but the anger and the poor therapy results of this session stand out, and I try to forget about it altogether. I lie down on my bed, exhausted although it is only 7 p.m., and turn on the radio. The phone rings, and one of my psychology colleagues is calling to ask if I have heard about Billy. I assume that he has either assaulted a staff member or attempted suicide. He has done both in the past. Instead I am told, "Billy escaped." I am wondering how, since security seems so tight. My colleague does not know, but assumes that someone did not do his/her job properly, and that the wily Billy took advantage.

I wonder if Billy will try to find me, either to seek help, since I am one of the few staff at the prison who gets along with him and is not totally turned off by his pathology, or to try to kill me for some alleged wrong. Billy sees people as wronging him, and while many have as he was growing up, including the uncle who raped him, many others have treated him well. But Billy is so full of anger, I do not know if he can accurately tell when people are helping him vs. hurting him. At times, he seems to have developed a paranoid world view, so that everyone is the enemy.

I go to the balcony and look outside, halfway expecting to see Billy. But it is dark. There are a few people around, but I cannot tell if any of them are him. Then, I reassure myself, thinking that it is unlikely that he would come here. For one thing, he probably does not even know where I live. But I cannot be sure.

My mind flashes back to another time when I tried to reassure myself about something. I got a chance to be a referee for a junior college basketball game. I had never done that before, but a friend of mine who was scheduled to referee the game did not want to do it and asked me to take his place. I agreed,

but later thought, "What if a fight breaks out?" The good ref-
erees race in among the players and break up the fight, seemingly not worried that they might get hit in the process. I
knew I did not want to race in and get a fist in the face, but I
did not want to be a bad referee either. I assured myself that
the chance of a fight occurring was small. But during the
game a fight actually did break out. I neither rushed in nor
ran off the court. I froze in one spot, and the players eventually broke up the fight. The other referee, who bragged to me
before the game that he had played football at Auburn, hur-
ried off the court when the fight happened.

I try to take my mind off things by watching the news on
television, but somehow the crime reports about homicides
seem more real than usual, and I am not reassured at all. I
decide to go to sleep. After what seems like a long time, which
includes thoughts of Billy, prison, and what it is like to suffer
pain, I finally fall asleep.

The Next Day

The alarm clock rings. I turn off the ugly sound, and realize it
is time to get ready or work. I wonder if I will hear more about
Billy or about how he managed to escape. The anticipation of
finding out these things makes the prospect of work better
than usual today.

When I get to the unit where our prisoners are, a few of
them are milling around. One comes up to me and says, "Did
you hear about Billy?" I say, "Yes, I heard that he escaped, but
I don't know any details. Do you?" He says, "I hear he paid off
some staff." But I think that such an explanation is unlikely
and probably the fantasy of this prisoner.

I run into Chuck, a guard nicknamed "Chuck Dog" by the
prisoners. It is in respect for his toughness. Prisoners respect
toughness and hate weakness. "Hey," says Chuck Dog, "Billy
left a note for you." He has it and I cannot wait to read it. But
it is a very disappointing note. No explanation really, no
threat, no nothing. Just a poorly written note, which looks like
that of a seven-year old, saying something like, "By the time
you get this I will be gone. I wonder if I will like it out there?
Time will tell." The only thing significant about this note is

that it was addressed to me. And the hint of his having become institutionalized: he wonders if freedom will appeal to him.

I start towards my office when I run into Hal, one of the more intelligent prisoners (most have below average IQs). He tells me, "Billy was talking about getting some people who deserve to be gotten. That guy could kill a lot of people. He is really angry." I debate whether to ask Hal if I am on the list. I chat some more, hoping he will tell me if I am, and if he knows it. Since Hal is not forthcoming with such information I say, "Are there any staff he has sworn to get?" and Hal says, "Not that I know of."

Cover-up

I am called into the office of one of the higher-ups in the prison administration. "Russell, we want you to change your reports on Billy to make him seem really dangerous." I tell him, "He is really dangerous." The administrator frowns and says "I know, but we have got to paint him as really very dangerous, in case he hurts people while he is out. We want to be able to say that we knew it all along. We are covering our ass here. Your job will be to go over all the things you wrote about him and put in more stuff about how dangerous he is, how he might kill people, things like that." I wonder if this is legal or proper, but my few questions are rebuffed. "Look" he says, "we are paying your salary, so do what we want."

I take the copies of the reports which he has given me. It is everything I have ever written about Billy: therapy notes, reports for the parole board, etc. How can I change them now? It does not seem proper. But I know the system here, and no defiance on the part of an employee is tolerated. I am between a rock and a hard place: do something which may be improper or illegal and satisfy the higher-ups, or stick to my principles and have a difficult time and maybe get suspended or fired. Or, at least, harassed like hell.

I make some feeble attempts at changing the reports and the next day I get a phone call. I assume they are going to ask me if I am making the changes, or to demand I finish up. Instead I am told that a new decision has been reached. They now think it better if we say he is not dangerous. After all, the prison was at fault in letting him escape, so it is better to emphasize that he is not all that bad. Then, if he kills someone on the outside or does something awful, it will seem like a momentary explosion on his part, and our fault in letting him escape will not seem so bad. So goes the argument. This is just as bad, if not worse, than the previous demand. I would rather elaborate on how dangerous he is, since I think he is potentially very dangerous. To have to write that he is not dangerous is a lie, and I feel worse than ever. Then, while I am still struggling with what to write, I get some good news, which makes the need for bogus reports moot.

Capture

I get the word at work. Billy has been captured in Montana. "Montana?" I ask, "What was he doing up there?" I am told he had an Uzi submachine gun on him, but the police initially spotted him from a helicopter and later got the drop on him by waiting behind some trees. When he was caught, Billy told them, "If you hadn't gotten me, I was going to kill a bunch of people." It could have been boasting, although the Uzi lends a degree of credibility to his threat.

Billy will not be sent back to our program. It was decided that since he escaped from here he needs a tougher, more secure setting. The only problem is that the place he is going to provides little or no therapy, and Billy could possibly profit from treatment. Also, society could profit if Billy could be turned around, since he could be made less of a danger to others. But it is not to be. Billy has sealed his fate with his escape and he is transferred to the tougher prison. Most people on the staff thought he was a hopeless case, anyway, and are glad to see him go. The guards are laughing about his new prison. "Billy was a tough guy here, but they are going to make a swishing queer out of him up there," one says. "Yeah," says another, "he is going to be someone's wife." The guards think this is very funny. I do not. Billy's problems began, in part, with his early sexual abuse, and now, in a horrible irony, he is going to be sexually abused again, if you can believe the guards' predictions. I see it as not funny at all.

Two Years Later

I am working in a university, having had all of the prison I could stomach. I am in the McDonald's across the street from the university, getting breakfast. I take the local newspaper off the restaurant rack, since I enjoy reading while eating. There is a guy a few seats away. He is very muscular with tattoos all over his arms. I think to myself, "I'll bet this guy is an ex-convict." I have to go to the bathroom. I have a fantasy that the ex-con will take my paper while I am in the bathroom, but I will come out and say, "Hey, punk, that's my paper." Either he will give it back, or he will want to fight. If the former, then the problem is solved, but if the latter I will beat the crap out of him. That is the fantasy. Nothing actually happens. The newspaper is still on my table when I return. But my fantasy is a little disturbing. I am thinking like the criminals I worked with in the prison. I tried to change them, but perhaps they changed me.

Afterword

In this chapter, originally intended as fiction but written with almost all fact, the only untrue part is the escape. Billy did not escape from prison. But everything else in the chapter is true.

Also, I WAS asked to change, in a dishonest way, my report about Billy, just as I describe. But, it was not to justify having someone who escaped, but to justify transferring him to a tougher, nontreatment program. I was told that my original, honest report contained too much about his pathology to justify having him transferred out of our treatment program.

Intelligent Behavior in Cats

by Russell Eisenman Ph.D. & Susan C. Eisenman

XOX XOX XOX XOX XOX XOX XOX XOX XOX XOX XOX XOX XOX XOX

Introduction

How smart are animals? Do they show intelligent behavior or just rote learning? Dingfelder (2008) reported that people may often read into the behavior of animals, attributing intelligence to them that the animal does not have. The following three examples of intelligent behavior in two domestic, long hair housecats, Thimble and Maxwell, would seem to show their intelligent behavior, well beyond mere rote learning. They were observed by the two authors, a Dad (first author) and his Daughter (second author) over a time period of 9 months, when Susan Eisenman moved from California and lived with Russell Eisenman.

Description of the Cats
(by the daughter)

Maxwell was a large black, male cat with white feet and was obtained from the Hayward, California Society for the Prevention of Cruelty to Animals (SPCA). He sure did not look like a stray, he was huge and healthy and with his sister. I felt bad taking him from his sister, but I already had Thimble (black and white in color) and wanted another cat. Thimble, a female, was a stray, obtained from the Alameda, California SPCA. She was tiny, and could fit in the palm of my hand. I always imagined Maxwell was some sort of reject show cat,

"Intelligent Behavior in Cats" by Russell Eisenman & Susan C. Eisenman.

like they felt his markings were not good enough so they gave him up. I do not know if that is true though. I might be biased about his beauty.

I used to go to a Mexican restaurant in Alameda and sometimes you would see stray cats walking around the rocks by the beach (when you sat in the outside area near the water). It was unusual to see cats and kittens near the ocean, to me it was anyway. I always thought I could imagine that Thimble was one of those types of cats. She was extremely adventurous. She climbed out onto the scaffolding of my Oakland, California apartment building when they were going to paint it. She hung from it like a monkey by one paw then made it back up, then she fell to the ground at one point. My neighbors found her in the garage with oil on her fur. She was always super curious.

Max was always very nervous. He always slept with me next to my pillow on one of my hands, but once in a while I would be sound asleep and wake to him hissing at me like a crazy cat, right in my face. I would use my pillow and covers to shove him off the bed. He would stare at me like I was evil. It was very weird. Not a fun way to wake up. I do not know if he had a bad dream or felt sick? I have no idea.

Thimble went totally nuts on the plane back to California when I was six months pregnant. She almost broke out of the box I was holding. She was like some person on PCP. It was awful. I think she got scared of the plane: did not like being confined and also may have had a bad reaction to the medication the veterinarian gave me to calm her. It was weird how no one near me seemed concerned that my cat was trying to break out of the box and totally nuts. I felt like I was in the twilight zone.

Max had white fur around his mouth like a goatee. He reminded me of some fancy dressed man in a tuxedo, so I wanted a name that fit that, so came up with Maxwell. I thought it sounded fancy. Thimble by the way, her name was after that ball of fluff I used to hold when I sucked my thumb as a kid. I always said I would name my first kitty of my own that name, and I did.

Intelligent Behaviors

1. Maxwell, the male cat, showed attempts at getting out of the house. He even learned how the doorknob worked and tried to operate it, although its construction prevented his paws from operating it. But, he developed a cognitive understanding, as shown by his standing on a chair to get to the doorknob, trying to turn the doorknob with his paws and trying to turn the lock level, in the middle, with his teeth. Neither his teeth nor his paws moved the doorknob, but he obviously had come to understand how they worked.

2. Maxwell and Thimble manipulated the first author to rub their head whenever they wanted it rubbed. The second author petted them but did not typically rub their head. When she moved to her Dad's house in Louisiana, the dad (the first author) rubbed their head frequently, while saying in a funny tone of voice "It's good, it's good, it's good." They repeatedly came to him to get their head rubbed, mostly while he was sitting in the living room chair facing the television set, where he first rubbed their head. Usually, he would give in and rub their heads (and repeat the words).

   But, on occasion he did not want to be interrupted in his television watching or book reading and he would not want to rub their heads. However each developed their own way to manipulate him, which was successful. Perhaps this speaks to sex differences. Maxwell would climb up on him and rub his head against Dad's hand. It was as if he was saying "Rub my damn head."

   Thimble, the female cat, on the other hand, would not climb up on Dad. Instead, she would wait expectantly, not moving, on the floor in front of him. If he still did not rub her head after several seconds, she would emit a plaintive, high-pitched cry, that Dad never heard before: "Eeeeeeee." In both cases, the cats got compliance, as Dad would rub their heads saying "It's good, it's good, it's good."

3. Dad suggested that the cats should have collars with nametags, in case they got out and got lost. Daughter bought such and we put them on the cats one evening. Their movements suggested they did not like having collars on. The next morning, they had gotten the collars off and arranged them, symmetrically, next to each other, a few feet from the door to the carport. It was as if they were saying "Take these collars and get them out of here." We never again tried to put the collars/nametags on them.

Discussion

The observations would seem to show intelligent behavior in the two cats. Both seem to have cognitive skills that help them get what they want, whether it is understanding how to open a door, manipulate a human to rub their heads, or rid themselves of the collars and show Daughter and Dad that the collars needed to be removed from the house. Thus, we conclude that the cats showed cognitive skills beyond mere rote learning.

Reference

Dingfelder, S. F. (2008, July/August). Fido's inner life. *Monitor on Psychology, 39* (7). Available at http://www.apa.org/monitor/2008/07-08/dogs.html

How We Think: Narratives

XXX XXX XXX XXX XXX XXX XXX XXX XXX XXX XXX XXX XXX XXX

Narratives are the stories we tell. From a radical standpoint, one could say that there is no reality, just narratives. Even without this radical position, one can appreciate the importance of the narrative as a way we communicate and think. In recent years, the study of narratives has increased, and there are now journals devoted to the study of the narrative.

From an evolutionary psychology viewpoint, the brain has evolved over the course of thousands of years. We know from historical findings that earlier cultures did not have the language or intelligence that we now possess. As a result, certain structures could be inherent in our language and thinking (Chomsky, 1972), that has helped us evolve language and thinking, and which could explain the narrative findings I am about to present.

Follow Up

Mortola (1999) drawing upon the writings of others in such areas as literature, cognitive psychology, philosophy, etc., suggests that there are three basic elements in narrative, that tend to follow in this order: equilibrium, disequilibrium, and modified equilibrium. The first part, equilibrium, is talk or writing about things being all right. The second part is communication about how the equilibrium has ceased, and things are now in a state of discord, called disequilibrium. The third part of a narrative would be modified equilibrium, in which some improvement is found. This improvement does not have to be a solution, but just an improvement over the second stage, disequilibrium. For example, the following communication would fit both the three elements and the alleged ordering of

---

"How We Think: Narratives" by Russell Eisenman.

the three elements of narrative: a person talks about their happy marriage (equilibrium), then how the marriage suffers and perhaps ends in divorce (disequilibrium), then how they are learning to deal with being divorced (modified equilibrium).

I was skeptical that narratives would necessarily have these three elements and would proceed in this way. So, I had video recordings of psychotherapy sessions analyzed, to see if the people in group psychotherapy followed the alleged narrative elements, and the alleged ordering (Eisenman, 2001). Eight students, three males and five females, participated in five group psychotherapy sessions for extra credit in their undergraduate psychology courses. One could argue that this is not "real" psychotherapy, but (a) the student patients seemed to take it seriously and revealed important things, and (b) from the standpoint of studying narratives, it does not really matter here whether we think of it as psychotherapy or as people telling stories. The therapists were one male graduate student and one female graduate student, who were doing the therapy as part of their graduate school training. Trained raters independently rated the statements made during the psychotherapy sessions, for the three narrative elements and the orders in which they occurred.

The findings were quite striking and are in accord with the idea that there is a tripartite structure to narratives. Overall, 51% of the statements by the patients followed the order of equilibrium, disequilibrium, and then modified equilibrium. The range was from 20% of the statements following this pattern, occurring in the second group psychotherapy session, to a high of 75% in the fourth group psychotherapy session. Thus, it would may well be that the evolved structure of our brains and our language lead to a particular tripartite pattern when we engage in narratives.

These findings are frightening, in the sense that they suggest that we perceive only a limited amount of what is going on, since we make it fit into a tripartite framework. As Pinker (1997) points out, there is an overwhelming possibility of what to perceive and think about. What is really happening "out there" is not tripartite, but our brains may only have evolved to the point where we can understand things in a tripartite fashion. Perhaps we have to limit our perceptions (Pinker, 1997) but to fit them into a tripartite mold is not necessarily the best way to understand our world and could lead to dangerous distortions.

References

Chomsky, Noam (1972). *Language and Mind*. New York: Harcourt, Brace, Jovanovich.

Eisenman, Russell (2001). The Three Alleged Elements of Narrative: Equilibrium, Disequilibrium, and Modified Equilibrium. *Journal of Evolutionary Psychology*, 22, 87-90.

Mortola, Peter (1999). Narrative Formation and Gestalt Closure: Helping Clients Make Sense of "Disequlibrium" Through Stories in the Therapeutic Session. *Gestalt Review*, 3, 308-320.

Pinker, Steven (1997). *How the mind works*. New York: Norton.

Conflict and Agreement in Sex Attitudes of Hispanic Male and Female College Students

XOX XOX XOX XOX XOX XOX XOX XOX XOX XOX XOX XOX XOX XOX

Possible conflict between Hispanic males and females in sex attitudes was found by Eisenman and Dantzker (2003). Further evidence was found by Eisenman and Dantzker (2006) and some of the results of that study are discussed here, along with additional insights.

Sex attitudes were studied in 330 university students from 10 undergraduate classes at the University of Texas-Pan American (UTPA), a Hispanic-serving university in deep South Texas, near the Mexican border (Eisenman & Dantzker, 2006). UTPA has more Mexican-American students than any other university in the United States. Males ($n=131$) and females ($n=199$) rated their level of agreement to 38 items on a 1-to-5 scale of a revised sexuality questionnaire developed by M. L. Dantzker and Russell Eisenman.

Evolutionary Psychology Theory

In recent years, evolutionary psychology theory has emerged as an interesting and important theory, especially useful in understanding sexual behavior of males and females (Barkow, Cosmides & Tooby, 1992; Buss, 1989, 1999; Eisenman, 2003, 2006). According to the theory, men and women have evolved different motivations due to their different biological realities. Men are motivated, ideally, to impregnate as many women as possible, in order to spread their genes to future generations.

From Julian Samora Research Institute Research Report #42, (Jan. 2009) by Russell Eisenman. Copyright © 2009 by Julian Samora Research Institute. Reprinted by permission.

Men are thus attracted to women with youth, health, and beauty. Since women become pregnant and cannot become pregnant again for nine months, a different strategy is needed. Women are thus attracted to men with money, status, and power, and are less interested in many sexual affairs, although they are not necessarily always monogamous. Women are also often attracted to men who will take care of them and their babies, whereas men put more emphasis on sexual intercourse *per se* as a major goal. These different motivations should lead to very different behaviors, at least at times.

Method

The revised 38-item sex attitudes test devised by M. L. Dantzker and R. Eisenman (Dantzker & Eisenman, 2005) was administered to 330 university students in 10 undergraduate classes at the University of Texas-Pan American, a Hispanic serving university that has the highest number of Mexican American students of any college in the United States. Males ($n=131$) and females ($n=199$) rated their level of agreement to 38 items on a 1-to-5 scale, on the sexuality questionnaire. There were 286 self-identified Hispanic students and 44 self-identified non-Hispanic students in the sample. We used t-tests to look for differences in mean scores (with the scores being the 1-to-5 ratings of each attitude item).

Results

Hispanic Males Compared to Hispanic Females

Of the 38 sex attitude questions, 23 showed statistically significant differences on t-test results between men and women. There were 10 items in which Hispanic males scored significantly higher (more agreement with the item) than did Hispanic females, and 13 items where Hispanic females scored higher (more agreement with item) than Hispanic males. The mean ratings of the 1-to-5 scale were as follows for the various human sex attitude questions, with *1=strong disagreement* and

5=*strong agreement*, with the mid-point 3=*doesn't matter*. The results are shown in Table 1.

Comparing Hispanics and Non-Hispanics

Since it may be that Hispanic culture is, in many ways, a conservative, religious one (often Catholic, or other conservative religions), it is important to know if Hispanic and non-Hispanic students disagree, or basically have the same sex attitudes. This next listing shows the attitudinal differences by ethnicity, i. e., Hispanic (males and females) vs. non-Hispanic (males and females). There were 19 statistically significant differences. In 10 instances, Hispanics agreed more with the sex attitude question, while in nine (9) instances non-Hispanics showed statistically greater agreement with a sex attitude item. The mean ratings of the 1-to-5 scale for Hispanics and non-Hispanics were as follows for the various human sex attitude questions, with 1=*strong disagreement* and 5=*strong agreement*, with the mid-point 3=*doesn't matter*. The results for this comparison are in Table 2.

Table 1.
Sex Attitudes of Hispanic Males vs. Hispanic Females

Attitude Means	Males	Females
(1) Premarital sex is acceptable for males.	3.39	3.09
(2) Premarital sex is acceptable for females.	3.13	2.82
(3) Oral sex before marriage is acceptable.	3.54	2.76**
(4) Oral sex is deviant behavior and should never be practiced.	2.07	2.48**
(5) Females should be virgins at the time of their marriage.	2.99	3.11
(6) Males should be virgins at the time of their marriage.	2.77	2.99
(7) A male should have some type of sexual experiences prior to being married.	3.18	2.53**
(8) A female should have some type of sexual experience prior to being married.	2.95	2.46**
(9) People should first live together prior to getting married.	3.21	2.93

(10) While growing up my parent(s) told me that premarital intercourse was unacceptable. 3.20 4.00**

(11) While growing up my parent(s) told me that any type of sexual behavior before marriage is unacceptable. 3.15 3.89**

(12) Sex should only occur with a person you love. 3.28 4.15**

(13) Sex and love are two different emotions. 4.22 4.11

(14) I always practice safe sex. 4.05 4.41**

(15) Any type of homosexual behavior is wrong. 3.31 2.67**

(16) Being bi-sexual is acceptable. 2.69 2.68

(17) Forcing a person to have sex is ok if it's your spouse. 1.58 1.40

(18) Having sex with an intoxicated person is rape. 3.49 3.53

(19) Once I get sexually aroused I usually have to have sex. 2.13 1.78**

(20) Being married shouldn't stop a person from having sex with someone other than a spouse. 1.96 1.39**

(21) Clubs that promote all "nude" dancing should not be allowed to exist. 2.23 3.14**

(22) "Topless Clubs" are acceptable places for adult entertainment. 3.60 2.69**

(23) Magazines like *Playboy* are demeaning to women. 2.40 3.47**

(24) Magazines like *Playboy* are pornographic material and should not be published. 2.19 3.27**

(25) Pornographic materials cause males to become sexually aggressive. 2.59 3.29**

(26) Pornographic materials have no affect on females' sexual behavior. 2.53 2.37

(27) Kissing should only take place between committed intimate partners. 2.28 2.56

(28) Kissing always leads to other sexual behaviors. 2.25 2.25

(29) It is the female's duty to take precautions against pregnancy. 2.40 2.45

(30) Condoms interfere with the pleasures of sex. 3.05 2.30**

(31) Masturbation is enjoyable. 3.62 3.09**

(32) Masturbation is wrong.   2.53   2.88*

(33) I would be jealous if my partner had sexual
     intercourse with someone else.   4.32   4.53

(34) Adultery of any kind should be illegal.   2.95   3.55**

(35) I would be jealous if my partner got
     emotionally involved with someone else.   4.33   4.44

(36) Sexual activities between two people of
     the same gender should be illegal.   2.96   2.64

(37) Anyone over 18 years of age should never
     have sex with someone under
     18 years of age.   3.04   3.52**

(38) Prostitution should be legalized in all states. 2.73   1.94**

---

*The difference between the means was statistically significant at .05.
**The difference between the means was statistically significant at .01.

Discussion

Men's Attitudes

The results show important areas of conflict in sex attitudes between Hispanic males and females. The males seem to endorse a life of freedom, at least for themselves. They are, however, anti-homosexuality, thus ruling out homosexuality for themselves. Probably, the vast majority are heterosexual and do not see this as a loss of any kind. They seem to want to have fun, and want things to be legal that will give them fun. They do not like the limitations of pleasure from condoms, and this makes me wonder if they would often have sexual intercourse without using condoms. If so, they are putting themselves and their partners at high risk of sexually transmitted diseases (Fierros- Gonzalez & Brown, 2002). Also, there is some evidence that people who engage in risky sexual behaviors also are more likely to engage in problem drinking and drug usage (Fleuridas, Creevy, & Vela, 1997). Overall, the men could be said to have permissive, liberal attitudes about sex.

Table 2.
Sex Attitudes of Hispanics vs. Non-Hispanics

Attitude Means	Hispanic	Non-Hispanic
(1) Premarital sex is acceptable for males.	3.19	3.59
(2) Premarital sex is acceptable for females.	2.93	3.41
(3) Oral sex before marriage is acceptable.	3.03	3.59*
(4) Oral sex is deviant behavior and should never be practiced.	2.34	2.03
(5) Females should be virgins at the time of their marriage.	3.07	2.81
(6) Males should be virgins at the time of their marriage.	2.91	2.52
(7) A male should have some type of sexual experiences prior to being married.	2.76	2.94
(8) A female should have some type of sexual experience prior to being married.	2.63	2.66
(9) People should first live together prior to getting married.	3.03	3.41
(10) While growing up my parent(s) told me that premarital intercourse was unacceptable.	3.72	3.66
(11) While growing up my parent(s) told me that any type of sexual behavior before marriage is unacceptable.	3.62	3.50
(12) Sex should only occur with a person you love.	3.84	3.56
(13) Sex and love are two different emotions.	4.15	4.13
(14) I always practice safe sex.	4.28	3.75**
(15) Any type of homosexual behavior is wrong.	2.90	2.53
(16) Being bi-sexual is acceptable.	2.69	3.56**
(17) Forcing a person to have sex is ok if it's your spouse.	1.47	1.35
(18) Having sex with an intoxicated person is rape.	3.52	2.94*
(19) Once I get sexually aroused I usually have to have sex.	1.90	1.72
(20) Being married shouldn't stop a person from having sex with someone other than a spouse.	1.59	2.00

(21) Clubs that promote all "nude" dancing should not be allowed to exist.	2.82	2.41
(22) "Topless Clubs" are acceptable places for adult entertainment.	3.01	3.41
(23) Magazines like *Playboy* are demeaning to women.	3.09	3.13
(24) Magazines like *Playboy* are pornographic material and should not be published.	2.88	2.44
(25) Pornographic materials cause males to become sexually aggressive.	3.04	2.84
(26) Pornographic materials have no affect on females' sexual behavior.	2.43	2.23
(27) Kissing should only take place between committed intimate partners.	2.46	2.55
(28) Kissing always leads to other sexual behaviors.	2.25	2.39
(29) It is the female's duty to take precautions against pregnancy.	2.43	2.13
(30) Condoms interfere with the pleasures of sex.	2.56	2.70
(31) Masturbation is enjoyable.	3.28	3.65
(32) Masturbation is wrong.	2.76	2.26*
(33) I would be jealous if my partner had sexual intercourse with someone else.	4.46	4.26
(34) Adultery of any kind should illegal.	3.34	2.74*
(35) I would be jealous if my partner got emotionally involved with someone else.	4.40	4.40
(36) Sexual activities between two people of the same gender should be illegal.	2.75	2.23*
(37) Anyone over 18 years of age should never have sex with someone under 18 years of age.	3.35	2.81*
(38) Prostitution should be legalized in all states.	2.22	2.65

*The difference between the means was statistically significant at .05.
**The difference between the means was statistically significant at .01.

Women's Attitudes

In contrast to the men, the women have more restrictive attitudes about sex, and favor censorship of certain sexual things, such as nude dancing or *Playboy* magazine. Their anti-oral sex attitude is particularly interesting, since most all professionals see oral sex as a natural part of a healthy sexual relationship. Part of the women's negative attitudes toward sex seems to relate to their upbringing, as shown by two items about what their parents told them about sex.

Thus, you have males who seem fun-seeking and willing to do lots of sexual things, and women who seem much more restrictive or conservative regarding sex. This would be expected to lead to conflicts between the men and the women, with each side seeing the other as strange with regard to attitudes and behavior regarding human sexuality.

In the case of a couple or potential couple, the male and female would have to negotiate their differences about sex, before being able to have a successful relationship. Even a well-negotiated or well-functioning relationship might face future conflict, as when the male starts reading sex magazines or wants oral sex and the woman sees these things as unacceptable.

It is possible that some of the conflict is more apparent than real. That would be the case if men and women have been socialized to think they are supposed to hold certain attitudes, but if their actual real-life behaviors are less rigid than what they say. Attitudes in Mexico have, historically, been changing from conservatism and male dominance to more liberalism and greater freedom for women (Corona-Vargas & Corona-Vargas, 2007). Possibly, my subjects may be showing, in part, the historical, stereotyped teachings of what males and females are supposed to think, but may be more flexible in their everyday life. In other words, their attitudes and behavior may reflect a combination of traditional teachings and more modern viewpoints.

Agreement Between Males and Females

While the obvious differences between the sex attitudes of males and females point to possible conflict between the sexes, there is also some evidence of agreement. On the one hand, there are all the attitude items on which they did not disagree to a statistically significant extent. But, even more revealing, perhaps, is that even when there were statistical differences, the differences were relatively small. Thus, the statistical differences were large enough to reach statistical significance, but small enough to indicate that there was lots of agreement between the Hispanic men and women. It was typically the case that men and women felt slightly different about some item, but not overwhelmingly different, even in the instances where statistical significance was obtained. Thus, it could also be said that men and women tended to feel the same about the items, even when there were statistically significant differences. For example, in only two items was there as much as a one-point difference between men and women. While the amount of difference was limited by having scores range only from 1-5 (*1=strong disagreement*, *5=strong agreement*), still the only two items that showed a difference of 1 or more were:

Magazines like *Playboy* are demeaning to women
and
Magazines like *Playboy* are pornographic materials and should not be published.

These items both had a difference of 1.07 and 1.08, respectively. The item "*Playboy* demeans women" received a mean rating of 2.40 from men and 3.47 from women. Thus, both of the following statements are true: women are more likely than men to believe that *Playboy* demeans women **and** both men and women are not especially likely to believe that *Playboy* demeans women. Likewise, the item that "Magazines like *Playboy* are pornographic materials" received a mean rating of 2.19 from men and 3.27 from women. Women are more likely to agree, but both are mostly disagreeing (men) or doesn't matter (women), since women are near the midpoint of 3.0 which we labeled "doesn't matter." In an earlier study we had originally called the midpoint "not sure," but many students crossed that out and wrote in "doesn't matter" (Dantzker & Eisenman, 2005). So, we realized that a better name for the midpoint, at least with Hispanic students at University of Texas-Pan American, was "doesn't matter."

Hispanics vs. Non-Hispanics

There were eight (8) statistically significant differences between Hispanics and non-Hispanics here, and several more in the Eisenman and Dantzker (2006) sample. Among the many findings, non-Hispanics were more likely to accept oral sex before marriage and being bisexual, while Hispanics tended to disapprove of many sexual behaviors in comparison to non-Hispanics. In general, compared to non-Hispanics, Hispanics come across as more conservative and restrictive regarding sexual practices.

The same point made about men vs. women can also be made about Hispanics vs. non-Hispanics. While there were many statistically significant differences, they are never large. So, it appears that Hispanics and non-Hispanics mostly agree about sex attitudes. Where there are differences the Hispanics come across as more restrictive, being somewhat against certain sex practices, at least more so than the non-Hispanics. But, there seems to be much agreement as far as the absolute means are concerned.

Sampling

It should be kept in mind that the subjects were college students, mostly Mexican-Americans. Thus, it is possible that research with other samples would yield different results (e. g., older subjects, people who did not go to college, Mexicans as opposed to Mexican-Americans, or people from other Hispanic regions of the country, etc.).

Conclusions

The results show many differences between Hispanic males and females and some differences between Hispanics and non-Hispanics. Generally, Hispanic males expressed more sexually permissive attitudes than Hispanic females, while non-Hispanics in general (gender not considered) expressed more sexually permissive attitudes than Hispanics in general (gender not considered). However, although there were many statistically significant differences, the amount of the differences tended to be small. Thus, there was much agreement, so it could be argued that Hispanic men and Hispanic women have much in common regarding sex attitudes and the same is the case between Hispanics and non-Hispanics. Overall, one could focus on the differences and say that many differences exist among Hispanic males and females that could result in problems between them. This is likely true for white, non-Hispanic men and women as well. However, the results show much agreement among the Hispanic men and women. Likewise, while there are a few areas of disagreement in human sexuality attitudes for Hispanics vs. non-Hispanics, they tend mostly to agree with one another. All the disagreements shown above are real, but they are not that great and there is also lots of agreement. So, the picture seems to be mostly one of agreement among participants rather than disagreement. While the disagreements should not be disregarded and future research could focus more intently on them, the reality of widespread agreement also needs to be appreciated.

The results both support evolutionary psychology theory and provide some problems for the theory. On the one hand, there were many statistically significant differences — especially the sex differences — that are consistent with the theory. Men seem to have a more permissive attitude about sex and women seemed to be somewhat more restrictive. The theory would predict this, although other theories, such as sex roles, could also predict it. On the other hand, the differences were small even when they were statistically significant.

Mostly, men and women agreed with one another, as did Hispanics and non-Hispanics. The disagreements were typically in instances where the participants had mostly the same attitude, but there might be slightly more agreement (or disagreement) between the two groups — males vs. females or Hispanics vs. non-Hispanics — regarding the degree of agreement/disagreement. Thus, the results, while showing some conflict mostly show agreement. The conflict is mostly consistent with evolutionary psychology expectations, but not as strong as one might have expected, given the emphasis in the theory on major differences between men and women.

References

Barkow, J. H., Cosmides, L. & Tooby,. J. (Eds.). (1992). *The adapted mind: Evolutionary psychology and the generation of culture.* New York: Oxford University Press.

Buss, D. M. (1989). Sex differences in human mate preferences: Evolutionary hypotheses testing in 37 cultures. *Behavior and Brain Sciences, 12,* 1-49.

Buss, D. M. (1999). *Evolutionary psychology: The new science of the mind.* Boston: Allyn & Bacon.

Corona-Vargas, E. & Corona-Vargas, A. (2007). Contrasts and contradictions: A brief look at the construction of sexuality in Mexico. In M. S. Tepper & A. F. Owens (Eds.) *Sexual Health: Vol. 3, Moral and Cultural Foundations* (pp. 229-241). Westport, CT: Praeger.

Dantzker, M. L. & Eisenman, R. (2005). Sexual attitudes among Hispanic students at a border university: Gender differences and failure to support Buss's jealousy theory. *Journal of Evolutionary Psychology, 26,* 71-80.

Eisenman, R. (2003). Forgetting to use birth control: Unwanted pregnancies support evolutionary psychology theory. *Journal of Evolutionary Psychology, 24,* 30-34.

Eisenman, R. (2006, November). Evolutionary psychology insights regarding human sexuality. *Europe's Journal of Psychology,* At: http://www.ejop.org/archives/2006/11/evolutionary_ps_1.html

Eisenman, R., & Dantzker, M. L. (2003, Summer). Possible Conflict in human sexuality attitudes between males and females at a Hispanic-serving university: Factor analysis of sexual attitudes. *Sincronia: A Journal of Cultural Studies.* At: http://sincronia.cucsh.udg.mx/eisenman203.htm

Eisenman, R., & Dantzker, M. L. (2006). Gender and ethnic differences in sexual attitudes at a Hispanic-serving university. *Journal of General Psychology, 133,* 153-162.

Fierros-Gonzalez, R. & Brown, J. M. (2002). High risk behaviors in a sample of Mexican-American college students. *Psychological Reports, 90,* 117-130.

Fleuridas, C., Creevy, K., & Vela, E. (1997). Sexual risk taking in college students and functional families of origin. *Families, Systems & Health, 15,* 185-202.